ENDORSEMENTS

"*Building Hope* is a wonderful reflection as to how one man, with God's help, can make a profound difference in this world. Dan Wallrath's story is both compelling and inspirational. His approach to helping others starts with one home renovation for a wounded warrior and builds to one hundred homes in a ten-year period of time. In today's society, we all must focus on not only helping ourselves but helping others as well. *Building Hope* gives us all a road map to follow to accomplish just that. Magnificent book."

– Lt. Gen. (Ret.) Rick Lynch, US Army

"Dan walks in rhythm with God's plan and purpose for his life, guided by the example of the Son. As you read the book, you will quickly come to know the limitless, untapped power that resides in each of us just beneath the surface of our outer being, waiting for a *yes* to God's will and calling. Mr. Wallrath's patriotic bent made him a perfect candidate for service to our wounded warriors. His genuineness comes through in every sentence, every word. We are fortunate he was chosen for this mission. And blessed he was not given peace until he said yes."

– Lt. Gen. (Ret.) Willie Williams, USMC

"Folks, Dan Wallrath is an American success story—a story where the good guy wins. We need more of these stories these days, when it sometimes seems that the 'bad guys' are winning. Dan has been helping to change a lot of lives for the better. Read all about it in his new book. I did."

– Larry Gatlin, country music singer/songwriter

"This book chronicles a journey of giving: how one man could hear a calling no one else did and how, in answering it, goes on a mission that miraculously puts people who share that vision with him on his path. The result changes lives for those soldiers and their families, who give of themselves for our freedoms."

– Victor Sansone, retired ABC Radio executive

"Dan Wallrath is a great American, period."

– Kid Rock

BUILDING HOPE

WHAT HAPPENS WHEN GOD
CHANGES OUR PLANS TO ACCOMPLISH HIS

DAN WALLRATH

BroadStreet
PUBLISHING

BroadStreet Publishing Group, LLC
Racine, Wisconsin, USA
BroadStreetPublishing.com

BUILDING HOPE: WHAT HAPPENS WHEN GOD CHANGES OUR PLANS TO ACCOMPLISH HIS

Copyright © 2016 Dan Wallrath

ISBN-13: 978-1-4245-5287-0 (softcover)
ISBN-13: 978-1-4245-5288-7 (e-book)

Stock or custom editions of BroadStreet Publishing titles may be purchased in bulk for educational, business, ministry, fundraising, or sales promotional use. For information, please e-mail info@broadstreetpublishing.com.

Cover design by Bruce Gore, Gore Studio, Inc.
Cover photograph by Paul Mobley, www.paulmobleystudio.com
Interior design and typesetting by Katherine Lloyd, www.theDESKonline.com

Printed in the United States of America
16 17 18 19 20 5 4 3 2 1

For the two most important women in my life—one who brought me into this world and loved and protected me when I needed it most and one who walked by my side throughout these many decades, loving and supporting me each step of the way. You have taught me to know God, to trust him as Father, and to lean into his plans for my life instead of my own.

Bettie Short and Carol Wallrath,
I love you both.

CONTENTS

FOREWORD

Three summers ago, I put on the uniform of an active duty United States Marine for the last time. It had been my attire every day for thirty-nine years straight, and as I buttoned up the jacket of my blues that final afternoon, I got a little sentimental over the whole deal. A major part of my journey was ending, and even though I was excited to see where things would lead in future days, I knew that most likely I'd never find the level of challenge, risk, fulfillment, or reward that I'd found in the US Marines.

As a military serviceman, I'd had both my basic needs met and a stabilizing sense of predictability day by day, neither of which I'd known as a welfare kid growing up in a single-parent home in Sumter, Mobile, and Hale Counties in Alabama—one of which is classified as the poorest county in the nation. I'd had the dignity of a meritocratic environment in which intelligence and effort instead of wealth and privilege were rewarded, a rarity for a black man coming up in the 1960s and 70s in "lower Alabama." I'd had the option to *thrive* in the US Marines . . . really, all I'd ever wanted in life.

Maybe it's all *anybody* wants in life, a conclusion I considered each time I welcomed another marine into my command. The more I'd learn of his or her story, the more I'd see how many read like my own. Those stories centered on overcoming great odds in order to achieve a bigger goal, a goal that always involved finding one's purpose in life, pushing beyond one's perceived limits, or being part of a team—or, in some cases, all of the above. "If something is God's, alone, to do," my adoring mother used to tell me, "then you let him do it. But if there is something any man can do, you can be that man." Despite the hardscrabble circumstances that tempted me to believe I'd never amount to anything, I had the audacity to believe my mom, and whenever I stood toe to toe with a marine fresh out of recruit training, I took the opportunity to pour that same sense of belief into them. In almost every case, they had the audacity to believe me, and they went on to achieve great things in their Marine Corps service as a result.

But here's the reality: war is war. It is always ugly. It is always unfortunate. There are always casualties found in its wake. Regardless of their preparedness, their willpower, or their perseverance when things got tough, some who signed up to protect our citizens' rights to life, liberty, and the pursuit of happiness were asked to sacrifice those very realities for themselves. They returned home from battle with injuries to their minds, their bodies, their spirits, or their souls and were thereby handed a new reality, a reality that paled by comparison to the strength and vitality they'd known before. Now unable to provide an income for their families, they then wrestled with their future, and with their worth. I often found myself shaking my head over the predicament; what could be done to help the heroes who had sacrificed so much for us? In 2012, my introduction to a tall, lanky Texas cowboy would start to answer that question for me.

I met Dan Wallrath when he and his wife attended a private dinner party hosted at the Home of the Commandants of the Marine Corps, and within moments of hearing Dan share his passion for building custom mortgage-free homes for wounded war veterans, I too was on fire for the vision. We swapped contact information at that gathering and stayed in touch. Within weeks of my retirement in 2013, Dan phoned to say that he was initiating a build in my new hometown—the first in the state of Alabama. Would I be willing to help him out?

I chuckled over his boldness and tenacity. No wonder the man got so much done!

The following month, a handful of Dan's team members and I convened in Alabama for the purpose of hosting a town hall meeting that would rally skilled craftsmen, builders, bankers, and others around the vision of building a home for a Marine who had served—and been injured—in Iraq. I explained our goal to those who had gathered and then stood there slack-jawed as person after person raised a hand to say, "I'll provide the wood," "I'll fund the lot," or "I'm in for the plumbing." We got that house built for pennies on the dollar, and Dan got himself a brand-new board member in me. Whatever the future held for Operation FINALLY HOME, I knew I wanted to be in on that.

What you will find in the pages to follow is the same spiritedness and stick-to-it-iveness I myself found, that first time I met Dan Wallrath. You will be moved by his story, I'll assure you; but more than that, you will be compelled to sort out what your role in the story is to be—not merely on behalf of wounded war vets (although given my background it won't surprise you that I'm especially partial to that group), but in terms of meeting needs *wherever* you may find them.

My hope for you is that this book is a wake-up call for you in the same way that it was for me—to catalog your gifts, talents, and experiences; to assess this present season of life; and to connect yourself to a cause that goes *beyond yourself* so that in your corner of the world, at least, hope gets bravely built.

Some things really are God's, alone, to do. But everything else? It's up to us. May we be found faithful to do our part.

Lt. Gen. Willie J. Williams, USMC (Ret.)
Huntsville, Alabama
June 2016

1

GLITZ, GLAMOUR, AND ONE STUNNED GOOD OL' BOY

SOME THINGS SEEM to go better together than others. Meat and potatoes. Boots and jeans. A pickup truck where the black tar ends. These things all make sense—versus, say, a Texas rancher in the heart of Hollywood, ambling along downtown L.A. streets. And yet in the fall of 2010, had you been seated at one of the myriad of open-air cafes or bistros that flank the area, you would have seen a tall drink of water wearing his signature black cowboy hat and oversize belt buckle move on by, something akin to an alien sighting in those parts, to be sure. I felt every bit as out of place as I looked.

My wife, Carol, and I were in town along with a few of our friends and family members for the filming of the fourth annual CNN *Heroes* tribute show, during which the news network honors individuals who are working to make a difference in their communities. It would have been enough to have been invited to *attend* a show like that, let alone be one of the honorees, but when I was told across a series of months that Operation FINALLY HOME, the organization that reflects both my spiritual calling and my lifeblood or passion, had been named one of the entries and then one of the top twenty-five contenders and then one of the top-ten finalists, I realized one of those seats of honor really was going to be for me. I felt humbled and anxious and proud.

The *Heroes* show was to air on Thanksgiving night, I was informed—could Carol and I be available the week prior, on November 20, for the filming? Without even checking with my wife, I told the producer yes. I was then given instructions regarding making our travel plans and reminded where to be and when.

The big event would take place at the legendary Shrine Auditorium, host site of countless awards shows—the Oscars, the Grammys, the Screen Actors Guild Awards, the People's Choice Awards, and more. The place has been around since the 1920s and across the decades has boasted pretty much every big-time music star, film star, and theater star known to humankind. I think it's also where Michael Jackson's hair caught fire during his filming of the commercial for Pepsi back in the 1980s. At least I'd be safe from that unfortunate turn of events, seeing as I'm bald.

Strangely at Peace

Upon arriving at The Shrine, I was flipped like a pinball, here and there and everywhere, from backstage to my seat in front of the stage and, ultimately, onstage. The setting was majestic. The air was abuzz with excitement, and CNN's production staff was totally on their game. Carol and I had been escorted along the red carpet with Hollywood notables Halle Berry, Demi Moore, Gerard Butler, Keifer Sutherland, Renee Zellweger, Marisa Tomei, LL Cool J, Jon Bon Jovi, and Jessica Alba. I was a long-tailed cat in a room full of star-studded rocking chairs and quite frankly should have been nervous to the point of vomiting. But for some reason, I felt at peace. "Even though you're going to be speaking to a worldwide audience numbering twenty million or more?" Carol asked. I just grinned and said, "Nah."

In reality, my wife's concern was warranted. Nine months prior, I had accepted a speaking invitation on a scale merely a fraction of what I was facing that night and had almost fainted dead away as a result of the countless butterflies calling my stomach home as I took the stage. Despite all the angst I'd had to overcome to finish out my talk before that bunch of homebuilders—hardly a terror-inducing audience—maybe the experience had somehow served to prepare me for what I was facing now.

The handlers they'd assigned to me and the other finalists were top-notch—attentive, understanding, and fully aware we were novices at all this. They walked our little group of newbies through the show's flow, telling us what to expect once cameras were rolling, how to deliver our remarks once each of our awards was presented to us, and the bail-out options available to us if and when we happened to flub (heaven forbid).

The main guy in charge looked at the lot of us once the housekeeping details were out of the way, and after exhaling meaningfully said, "Folks, you ten were selected from an initial pool of more than ten thousand submissions from more than one hundred countries. You ought to be very proud of yourselves. Whatever else happens here tonight, enjoy yourselves."

Sounded like a good plan to me.

The One Thing I Could Do

Once Carol and I were shown to our seats and I had a moment to catch my breath, settling into the situation a little, my attention turned to the nine other heroes being honored that night. Anuradha Koirala, a Nepalese woman adorned in a colorful dhoti that night, was rescuing girls out of sex-slave trafficking by taking them in, even the ones clearly dying of AIDS, and raising those young women as her own. A Scottish man, Magnus MacFarlane-Barrow, had founded a charity called Mary's Meals that fed nearly half a million starving people in Africa every single day. Kentucky-born Harmon Parker built footbridges spanning crocodile-infested waters all over sub-Saharan Africa, providing safe passage over flood zones and connecting isolated communities one to another. His bridges allowed residents means for getting to the clinic or to the market even when waters were high, but more importantly, those bridges were saving lives. Harmon's parents both died in a flash flood in Kenya, a colossal loss that most likely would have been prevented had one of his bridges already been built.

The stories went on and on. For my part, although seeming to pale by comparison when stood up next to the significant contributions of the men and women seated around me, it was with the same determination to help hurting people that I'd started Operation FINALLY HOME five years prior. Since America's War on Terror began, following the devastating events of 9/11, more than 2.5 million troops have been deployed to Afghanistan and Iraq, and more than sixty-six hundred of them haven't made it back alive. That latter stat equates to almost four thousand women and men who were widowed as a direct result of the war, either because of death through combat or via accidental causes—and those numbers didn't even factor in death from suicide, a whole separate and tragic stat. Almost two thousand of our military men and women returned with injuries requiring amputation and, therefore, an entire swath of lifestyle changes as they grew accustomed to compromised mobility, and a staggering fifty-two thousand and counting have been wounded in action—never a benign effect.[1]

I wasn't a military man myself and had no real ties to our country's armed forces, but in a decade significantly defined by our nation's repulsion for terrorism, and thus a firm commitment to continue sending troops into harm's way, only a simpleton could miss the realities our returning fighters faced once they eventually made their way home. I'd been a custom homebuilder my entire adult life, and while I couldn't provide prosthetics for soldiers' amputated limbs, treatment for their horrific PTSD episodes, or reassurance that their valiant contribution would in fact help end the war, what I could provide on the heels of their having to endure tearful departures from loved ones, challenging travel halfway across the world, grueling conditions living in the desert, and the unparalleled stress of being "at war" twenty-four hours a day was a beautiful and inviting place for them to call *home*.

As I relaxed into the plush theater seat, I reflected on the journey Operation FINALLY HOME had been on thus far. The fruit of its labor felt less like an entrepreneurial endeavor and more like an unexpected adventure, less like a corporation and more like a divine calling. And in the midst of the bustling activity, more than six thousand guests made their way into the auditorium, and official-looking crew members finalized details for the production, while I quieted my mind for a few minutes before God and thanked him for including me in this event. Regardless of what some list with my name on it said about me, and even in light of the extraordinary work my comrades were doing all across the globe, I knew in my heart that my heavenly Father alone was the truest hero here.

My attention was thrust back into the event at hand when CNN anchor Anderson Cooper took the stage, master of ceremonies for the evening. Soon enough, Kid Rock was standing before

Kid Rock and Dan Wallrath at CNN *Heroes* show

the audience, inviting us all to watch a preproduced video segment about Operation FINALLY HOME, part of his introduction of me as a top-ten *Heroes* finalist. Carol reached for my hand, and together, we absorbed the images being projected for all to see. Surreal and sweet—no other way to describe it. The video wrapped, and Kid Rock was flooded once again in spotlights, there at center stage. "Please join me in welcoming Mr. Dan Wallrath, founder of Operation FINALLY HOME," he said with a wide smile. I stood, buttoned my sports coat, and strode toward the stage. It was only after I'd ascended the few steps, accepted the handsome trophy from the charming and talented man (who for some reason liked to be called "Kid"), and turned to face the audience that I realized they were all standing too. And applauding. Loudly. A distinct lump formed in my throat.

The crowd eventually settled down and sat down, cueing me to begin my short speech. Teleprompters were all over the place, each one rolling slowly through my preplanned opening remarks, but here, in this moment, in front of the watching world, the words I'd scripted for myself didn't seem like the right words to say at all. *Just read the script, dummy!* I heard my better judgment scream inside my head, even as I launched headlong into an entirely different speech.

Divine Intervention on the Disney Bus

My problem in that onstage moment stemmed from the fact that one of the friends I'd invited to accompany Carol and me to the awards show that night was US Marine Corps Staff Sergeant Scott Worswick. He and his wife, Heather, were living in a home built by Operation FINALLY HOME, and their story perfectly encapsulated our organization's mission, vision, and values.

I'd met Scott by sheer coincidence—his family and my wife and I happened to be on the same commuter bus at Disney World in Orlando, all of us weary after a day at the theme park. Carol and I were in town for a conference but had decided to hop over to Disney in order to purchase a few Christmas presents for our grandkids. We'd spent several hours shopping amid the always-present throng of parents and their young children, and we were ready for a break from the stimulation and a quiet ride back to our hotel. But that wasn't to be. As our bus pulled away from the stop, I couldn't help but take an interest in the young family approaching curbside from the rear. I was about to say something to the driver, when he noticed them on his own and lurched to a stop. Moments later, a young father came hobbling up the bus's few steps, carrying a cane while trying to manage both a toddler and a large stroller. His wife trailed him, an infant wriggling in her arms and a second stroller in tow. It looked like a novice circus: this bedraggled family and all their gear. Either this was going to take forever or someone was going to fall down and get hurt. I reflexively jumped up to help, reaching for a stroller with one hand and a diaper bag with the other, and helped them get settled into seats. Despite there being nobody else on the bus, they opted for seats right next to us—an answer to prayer, I'd soon find out.

I struck up a casual conversation with the man—he told me his name was Scott Worswick—which is when I discovered that he and Heather were in town for the very same conference Carol and I were attending. It was a series of seminars for wounded veterans; deducing the obvious, I thanked Scott for his service to our country and asked about his cane.

During a tour of duty in Iraq in 2004, Scott was part of a routine convoy when his vehicle hit a roadside bomb. He suffered a resulting concussion and such major back trauma that the eighteen surgeries he'd already undergone hadn't adequately fixed his problem. Docs had to fuse several of his vertebrae to his spine just to enable the most basic ambulation for him. The story leveled me, but what was more profound was the countenance on his face as he laid out the events. He spoke with such pride in his unit that my chest puffed out a little just by association. "I am happy I was able to serve," he said with a broad smile.

Scott Worswick, Staff Sergeant (SSgt), US Marine Corps, and family with Texas Governor Rick Perry

Scott Worswick, SSgt, and family with Governor Rick Perry

In that moment, I was as proud of Scott Worswick as I would have been of my own blood kin.

Scott told me he was from southern Florida but was hoping to relocate to Houston for better job opportunities, now that he was medically retired. He and Heather were on a fixed income though. Given that, how could a move happen?

What Scott couldn't have known was that I was a homebuilder on a mission to build homes for people just like him. I began to explain to Scott the tenets of my organization and asked him if he'd like to apply for a home. Taking a very brief detour from the path of straight-up honesty I usually practice, I told the hopeful couple that it was a long shot that they'd get into one of our homes, that there was quite a vetting process at work, and that it could take some time before a decision was made.

In fact, I was 100 percent sure my team and I would be building the Worswicks a new home that year. I'd asked God to cross my path with a veteran in need, and God had laid this amazing soul almost literally right in my lap. Done.

Later that night, at the conference's closing dinner, I approached the Worswicks to invite them to sit at our table. Our conversation went deeper this time as Scott opened up about not just the physical struggles he'd endured upon returning home but also the emotional, spiritual, psychological, and practical ones. Daily life was proving quite the challenge for him, given his constant, pervasive pain. He didn't harp on these issues, but each time he adjusted his position in his chair, I noticed him struggle and wince. Despite all the candid insights he'd offered, I got the feeling things were much harder for my new friend than he was letting on.

The Real Heroes

Back at the CNN *Heroes* show, when I was supposed to be rattling off my electronically prompted speech, I had glanced down at Carol and in my periphery caught sight of Scott. I trained my gaze on him then, and that's when all bets were off. "Folks, it is quite an honor to be called a 'hero' before you all tonight," I started, "but let me tell you about one of the real heroes I know. Believe it or not, there are ordinary men and women, just like you and me, who voluntarily raise their hands and say, 'I'll go. I'll fight for our country's freedom. I'll even die, if it comes to that, to protect what is our sacred trust.'"

Glancing at the teleprompters, I noticed they'd all been shut off. Nothing but black screens surrounded me; I was officially on my own now, flying with no safety net.

I motioned toward the man in dress blues seated in the front row and continued. "My friend here, Marine Corps Staff Sergeant Scott Worswick, has endured close to twenty surgeries on his back and is facing another half dozen in future days. The man has more steel in his back than I do in my pickup truck. And yet his heart still beats with pride for this country, for our armed forces, and for his investment even at grave expense. This award is for saints like this soldier. Thank you for your service, Scott."

The crowd stood and cheered, a completely appropriate response to Scott's heroism. I tipped my cowboy hat toward him, scanned the crowd to take in the moment honoring my friend, and closed with, "God bless you, and God bless America."

The award in hand, I was ushered backstage so the next presentation could be made, which is when I ran into Kid Rock again. He reached out to shake my hand and said, "I'd like to get involved with what you're doing, Dan." Assuming he was just caught up in the emotion of the moment, I thanked him and said on a whim, "That would be great! Maybe we could partner on something in your hometown of Detroit," a detail I possessed only because I'd googled him days before the show.

He flashed a genuine smile, told me he'd like that very much, and strode past me to wherever he was going next. I honestly thought I'd never hear from him again. Boy, was I ever wrong. If I'd ever wondered about God having a sense of humor, the eventual flourishing of a relationship between a world-renown megawatt rapper/rocker and me, a good ol' boy from south Texas, would certainly clear things up.

Ready to Retire

The road to The Shrine, when twenty million people were exposed to the work of Operation FINALLY HOME and our tiny organization was thrust into a stratosphere of opportunity we'd never known, was paved with a lot of old-fashioned stick-to-it-iveness and sweat. With nothing more than a high-school education and an appreciation for scrappiness, I'd side-jobbed my way into business ownership. During my growing-up era, my father had been involved in the homebuilding industry, and at some level, every gig putting in air-conditioning units or framing houses during those teenage-year summers was an effort to make him proud. I liked working with my hands, and the skills came easy for me; by twenty-three, I'd signed on with my father to help him run his freshly minted window-manufacturing business and quickly was impressed by the hefty paychecks yielded by hard work.

I stuck with Dad's firm for eight years before my steadied confidence and industry acumen beckoned me to do my own thing.

At some level, I'd always wanted to build homes, and so eventually that's what I did. On January 14, 1981, I filed official documents with the Texas Secretary of State declaring Classic Builders, Inc., a bona fide firm.

Classic eventually became "Dan Wallrath Custom Homes," an endeavor that had a great run across the decades of its charmed existence, but by the spring of 2005, Carol and I were entertaining the idea of retirement. I was fifty-three years old, Carol and I had been married nearly thirty-five years, our two grown sons both were married and thriving in their respective fields, and we were months away from welcoming our fourth grandchild to the mix—numbers that all seemed to add up to taking a load off and resting up a bit. We wouldn't coast exactly: my business would still need a figurehead, we were highly invested in social activities with several close friends, and our various church involvements weren't going anywhere. We'd just reached a point when we were ready to settle down, build our "forever-after house," and quit doing the thousand things each day that running a business required.

I stacked up all my reasons for veering toward retirement like logs on a fire and wasn't surprised in the least when Carol came along with a can of fuel. As a homebuilder's wife, she'd never had a house to call her own. In the same proverbial vein as a cobbler's children never having shoes, custom homebuilders are serial stewards of houses they've built and now live in, but only until a viable buyer comes along. Your home is always for sale, which means your interior always needs to be "staged." Suffice it to say, during the years when our kids were young and messy, this reality didn't exactly equate to a stress-free marriage. What's more, during her growing-up years Carol's dad was a marine who then accepted a call into ministry, both highly transient roles. In her words, after all these decades of moving around, she was "ready to stay put." What neither of us realized at the time was that in spite of our thoughtful rationale, God wasn't at all on board with our plans for retirement. To lean into the state verb of Texas, our heavenly Father was fixin' to throw a big wrench into our well-crafted plans.

The Course-Correcting Call

Several weeks after our discussion about the prospect of retiring, I received a phone call from Joe Baucus, a salesman who often sold me the windows I installed in the custom homes I built. We talked on a fairly regular basis, so it wasn't out of the ordinary that he reached out. What proved to be unusual was the nature of his call. He wondered if I would entertain a remodel project on behalf of a friend of his. I was formulating my decline to Joe's offer—I didn't have time for remodel jobs given the full-scale builds my company did week after week—when I heard him say, "Dan, I know this isn't customarily your approach, but please hear me out."

Joe went on to explain that his friend Steve Schulz's twenty-year-old son Steven, a marine who had served in Iraq, needed his home remodeled to accommodate injuries he had sustained while overseas. Evidently, Steven's Humvee had run over a roadside bomb—an improvised explosive device or IED—and now

Stephen Schulz, Lance Corporal (LCpl), US Marine Corps, after injuries

the young man was wheelchair-bound and soon returning to a home with tight passageways all throughout. Steve and his wife were willing to do whatever they could in order to get their house outfitted for their son, even as they were dealing with limited financial resources and a time crunch: if all went as expected, Steven would be discharged from National Navy Medical Center in Maryland (now known as Walter Reed National Military Medical Center) in a matter of weeks.

Stephen Schulz, LCpl,
before injuries

"When Steve told me about this situation," Joe continued, "your name was the first name that popped in my head."

I was honored by Joe's consideration, even as I doubted I was the right resource for the job. I decided I'd just take an hour and go meet Steve and his wife, maybe put them in touch with a good remodeler I happened to know. I felt sure the guy would cut Steve a deal, given the harrowing story involving his son.

A Planner without a Plan

At an appointed time later that week, I knocked on Steve Schulz's front door and was warmly welcomed in. After exchanging pleasantries, Steve handed me a photo of his son, taken before Steven had sustained the IED injuries. I saw in the frame a strapping young man full of vitality and strength, standing with his arms folded across his chest in something of a hero's pose. He had biceps that had to be seventeen inches in circumference and an adventurous sparkle in his eye, like the kind of kid who lived life to the fullest. Then, Steve showed me an "after" picture, taken recently by hospital staff, a sight that wrenched my heart and caught my breath. This young man was thin. Frail. Squinting at the camera with an uncertain gaze. My eyes filled with tears as I tried to piece together how it was possible that this was the same person I'd seen in the first shot. I must have glanced plaintively at Steve because he began putting words to the severity of his son's trauma. "He's literally half the man he was," Steve said. "He slumps down in his wheelchair all day long, unable to hold himself up. It's the head injury, Dan. What I mean is my son will never fully function again."

Steve's wife, Debbie, a public school teacher, had taken time off from her job so she could remain at her son's side in Bethesda this entire time, but the financial toll of her unpaid leave was putting quite a strain on the family. I would learn this was only the beginning of a long road ahead; given Steven's prognosis—"He will need constant care, twenty-four hours a day"—the doctors had told Debbie the financial burden was only beginning. "We either need to sort out a remodel," Steve was saying to me, "or else bite the bullet and arrange for Steven to live in a special home where they have staff who are equipped to tend to his needs."

Debbie was willing to resign from teaching and be trained to be Steven's fulltime caregiver, but there was still the issue of the remodel. A quick glance around my surroundings told me that wheelchair accessibility was only the first in a long line of needs. Carpet would need to be replaced with tile, countertops would need to be lowered, every bathroom would need a major overhaul, and more. Steve mentioned he was willing to take out a loan, but he wasn't sure what he would qualify for. "The VA is willing to give us about five grand," he said, which only worsened the headache I'd felt come on. My mental tabulations were hovering around forty or fifty thousand dollars, and these were conservative estimates, given everything that needed to be done. What was this family supposed to do?

I'm a man who prizes a plan—always have been. And yet, while standing in the Schulzes' living room with a man I'd only moments before met and with nothing even approximating a plan for how to move forward, I stuck out my hand and said, "Mr. Schulz, I'd be honored to take on this job."

Twenty minutes later, I was sitting behind the wheel of my

truck, which was still parked in the Schulzes' driveway, wondering what on earth I'd just done.

Holy Work

From my first days of involvement in the building industry in the 1970s, I had availed myself of the opportunity to join and, in some cases, lead builders' associations on the local, state, and national levels. It was a great way to connect not just with other builders but also with bankers, developers, suppliers, contractors, electricians, plumbers—everybody who had anything whatsoever to do with the homebuilding industry, nationwide. Relationships went deep quickly; we all were vested in the same types of interests and valued means for making our business dealings more efficient and more effective.

The local association—known as BABA, or the Bay Area Builders Association, which is a subsidiary of the Greater Houston Builders Association—would become a crucial partner for me as I sought to pursue God's call on my life. In fact, on the afternoon that I drove away from the Schulzes' home, I began rattling through my mental Rolodex of fellow BABA members,

BABA Team

intent on finding anyone and everyone who could help me accomplish the remodel for Steven. I simply could not let this family down. Across the years, I'd worked with every lumberyard, plumbing outfit, and electrician in the greater Houston area—surely some of them would pitch in. I'd call in every favor. I'd barter for cut-rate materials. I'd smile and dial and share this story until every last to-do box was checked.

In the end, every breath of effort paid off. Astoundingly, not a single request was refused; in fact, quite the opposite scenario occurred. Time and again, as providers and suppliers offered up free labor and materials, they thanked me for letting them join in.

Within four weeks, my ragtag team of do-gooders and I had completely remodeled the downstairs master bathroom, installing a roll-in shower and lower vanity, both of which would accommodate Steven's wheelchair. We had ripped out every fiber of carpeting and laid in brand-new tile in its place, and we had widened interior doorway openings and installed ramps to abut exterior doors. Steven's reaction to seeing his family's remodeled home summed it up for me, once everything was said and done: "I feel human again," he said with a subtle grin. Every person deserves as much.

Our work may have been quick and dirty, but still it was highly professional, which is what you get when you assemble a group of experts who are passionate about the cause. In terms of project efficiency, it wasn't lost on me that to date it was the smoothest build I'd ever been part of. Furthermore, it was completed at zero cost, both to the family and to our team. God clearly was up to something here.

Soon after the completion of the Schulz build and spurred on by that gnawing sense that I'd stumbled my way into undeniably holy work, I went back to my BABA colleagues with a challenge: "We're all homebuilders," I told them at our next scheduled meeting. "We need to find another wounded veteran and build him or her an *entire* home. Mortgage-free, totally custom, all the bells

and whistles—a place for a hero to call home." I choked up a little as I cast my vision, but I plowed ahead, boldness and passion
leading the way. We shouldn't hang our hats on the remodel, I
told the other members. We needed to stretch our faith and work
to bless more men and women who put their lives on the line for
us every day.

The BABA board's decision was unanimous that day. Eight
for eight, they were all in.

Within a matter of weeks, my builder pals and I had located
the recipient of our first full build, twenty-two-year-old Lance
Corporal Chris LeBleu—"Blue," his fellow marines called him—a
calm, resilient rifleman who was part of a company charged with
protecting a base near Syria. He had returned home safely to his
wife, Melanie, in September 2005, and eagerly anticipated their
building a long, happy life together. Chris had no way of knowing
that he brought home more from Iraq than memories of war; lurk-
ing within his cells was a deadly virus thought to have been picked
up from drinking contaminated water or breathing toxic fumes.
By Christmas, Chris' liver was so weakened that he could barely
eat food or drink water without becoming ill. Soon thereafter, he
became jaundiced and incoherent, which is when doctors placed
him on life support. Chris needed a new liver and fast.

Against the odds, days later Chris and Melanie were informed
that a liver had been located. Surgery was scheduled, and while
the couple rejoiced over the life-sparing turn of events, a long and
arduous road of recovery still lay ahead. Melanie would need to
quit her job in order to transport Chris to daily medical appointments for the foreseeable future. To complicate matters further,
once Chris was discharged from his weeks-long post-op stay at the
hospital, he and Melanie would need to relocate from their current
apartment to a near-sterile environment that was totally free of
toxic molds and mildew, if Chris stood any chance of recovering
from his transplant surgery.

As more and more information surfaced on this couple, my

wheels couldn't help but spin. "Hmmm," I said to my BABA partners in crime, "I wonder if this couple could use a brand-new home
located in close proximity to the Houston Medical Center . . ."

And so we built. And then we all had the bug to build more,
which is when I begged God to lead us to another recipient and
days later met Scott and Heather Worswick on that Disney World
transit bus. We'd completed the Worswicks' build too, a home
worth more than $200,000 that we managed to complete for just
under thirty grand. A few industry naysayers had had the audacity
to tell me that it was an "impossible goal," but I knew better. I
figured if God was behind all this business, then he would make
impossible things possible along the way.

I inhaled deeply as I summoned the courage to tell my beloved
Carol that retirement would have to wait.

Leave a Legacy You Love

NOW IT'S YOUR turn. At the end of each chapter, you'll find
a handful of questions and considerations to help you locate your
calling and build a legacy you'll be proud of. I hope you'll take
advantage of these opportunities to think through the themes presented and sort out what they mean for your unique personality,
experience, talents, circumstances, challenges, and dreams.

1. When have you experienced an abrupt change in life-
   plans that at the time made no sense to you? Have you
   ever considered that the shift might have been divine
   intervention of some sort? Why or why not?

2. For me, the dramatic shift was definitely "of God" and
   now is something I view as my primary purpose in life—
   my "calling," if you will. How would you define your life's
   calling? In other words, what type of involvements fuel

you, fill you up, and keep you motivated for fighting the good fight in this world? (If you don't yet know what your calling is, hang in there with me. We'll sort it out together across the chapters to come.)

3. After I got over the shock of having my retirement plans thwarted, I almost immediately accepted the new path I was on as a grand adventure—a posture that has served me well. Do you tend to view new frontiers, new directions, new perspectives, and new paths more as disruptions to minimize or as adventures to be seized? What life experiences, assumptions, fears, or insecurities do you suppose factor into your attitude here?

4. I mentioned that, initially, Carol wasn't exactly thrilled by the prospect of my pursuing the work with Operation FINALLY HOME. She wanted to *settle down* and not *gear up* for another series of changes. How do you think you'd respond if you felt "called" to do something meaningful for God and yet didn't receive quick support from the loved ones in your life?

5. At the close of the chapter, I admitted that while I certainly didn't have the answers as to how my calling was going to work out, I knew that God would make impossible things possible somehow. When have you seen God show himself strong in a moment of your weakness? How did the experience shape your view of God?

2

DIVINELY CALLED (I THINK)

FOR ME, CHURCH involvement began as a result of my extended family's influence. My dad's parents and my mom's grandparents lived within walking distance of our tiny home in Indiana, and on occasion either my grandmother or my great-grandma would extend an invitation to my siblings and me to come to church with her. Their husbands were around but not really interested in spiritual matters; they outsourced that part of family life to their wives, figuring the women would handle things just fine.

Neither of those family members owned a vehicle, and so on appointed Sunday mornings, my older brother, my three younger sisters, and I would head out on foot to one of their houses, and then together we'd walk to church, either to the little Baptist one up the road or else the other one, which if memory serves was Church of Christ. Regardless of which church we attended, I remember liking the safety of that environment. I liked the rhythms and rituals, the predictability of the order of service, the belted-out hymns, and the talk of a place of peace after death for those who knew and trusted Christ.

My home life was extremely dysfunctional, courtesy of my dad's proclivity for alcohol and physical abuse, and with five kids to raise and a lot of chaos to manage in her marriage, Mom always had her hands full, just trying to survive. The little money my dad made he used to fund his drinking habit, which is why nearly every evening my brother, Mike, and I would head out to scour ditches in search of Coke bottles that had been tossed aside. Each bottle equated to two pennies, according to our state's bottle-deposit program, and while I can't tell you how much I paid for my last vehicle, I can tell you that when I was a young boy, a bag of beans cost exactly nineteen cents. Mike and I would hunt and hunt until we'd found ten glass bottles, which would get us a bag of beans for Mom to cook up for dinner and a penny profit to boot.

In an effort to help make ends meet, my mother often picked up shifts at the local grocery store—anything a high-school educated woman could do—and sometimes Sunday morning found her unpacking cartons or stocking shelves, instead of relishing the luxury of taking her kids to church. That would have been a dream come true for Mom, having an intact family that prized the practice of attending church. But that particular dream wasn't to be. Because of my father's poor decisions, a lot of my family's dreams weren't to be.

Getting Along with God

I met Carol during my high-school days—she was a year behind me in school—and quickly after that first meeting, I knew that she was the one. I was all of sixteen years old, but Carol's steadiness and beauty were so attractive to my wounded body and heart that I pursued her with everything I had, a wayward star in search of an orbit to call its own.

Everything about Carol was perfect: her look on life, her attitude, and her family—especially her family. Carol's dad pastored a small church, and her mom worked to help that ministry salary stretch to the days in a given month. At her father's insistence, Carol and her two sisters would straighten up the house and make sure everything was in order each evening while her dad would prepare a cup of hot coffee for her mom, so that upon her arrival

Mom could spend her first few minutes just relaxing. None of it computed with me, given the father figure I'd grown up with. A six-foot-three former marine with a deep and commanding voice made a practice of waiting on his *wife*? I'd never heard of such a thing. *Women* were to serve *men*, not the other way around—that much I knew to be true. Or so I'd been taught, anyway.

Carol's father pastored in the town of Galena Park, a small outpost that ran just north of the Buffalo Bayou portion of the Houston Ship Channel, where my father had relocated our family when I was ten years old. Early in Carol's and my relationship, he looked at me and said, "Dan, if you want to take my daughter out on Saturday nights, then let's get one thing straight: You *will* be in church on Sunday mornings." He was smiling as he said those words, but I knew he meant business. Still today, whenever I have the opportunity to speak to men—at church gatherings, at retreats, at business meetings, and so forth—I remind them of the influence they have over the young men who want to court their daughters. I will forever be grateful that Carol's dad exerted his influence with me. At his insistence, I showed up every Sunday morning to hear his preaching, and by age seventeen, I had surrendered my life to the lordship of Christ.

For some people—especially those who suffer abuse at the hands of their earthly father—accepting the idea that there is a heavenly Father who is loving and gracious and forgiving and generous and kind can be a really difficult pill to swallow. They think back to the countless episodes when their dad told them they were worthless or when their dad struck their face in anger or when their dad withheld affection as a means for punishment, and they just can't make this idea add up. When I began my relationship with God, I was similarly perplexed. Carol would explain to me that God the Father would never hurt me, strike me, shame me, or call into question my worth, to which my brain would all but short-circuit. *The father I know doesn't behave at all like that.*

It would take years of Carol's patient insistence that God's love was real before I could wear that reality like a custom-fitted suit, but eventually I got there. Eventually, I learned she was right.

Still, I suffered periods of confusion whenever I'd reflect on scenes from my youth. There was my brother, Mike, age sixteen—just two years older than I was—having upset our father for one reason or another and now being yanked toward the garage, where my father would pick up a board and begin to strike him. There I was, inside the house but now horrifically aware of violent strikes and whimpers riding on airwaves right to my ears. There was my father, once again having turned monstrous, unsuspecting of my arrival with a baseball bat in hand. The strikes against my brother ceased as my wild swings struck the air all around my dad, and then there I was fleeing the scene, running for my life, knowing that in his enraged state my father would literally kill me that day, a rabid animal senselessly ripping apart its prey.

I'd flash back to a scene like that and through weeping ask, "Why, God? *Why?*" To which, in lieu of direct and logical answers, he'd simply assure me he was near.

Mom and Dad would divorce when I was twenty-three years old, my father finally deciding that his adulterous affairs over the years weren't as satisfying to him as leaving my mom for good surely would be. And I remember thinking that in the same way I'd married Carol at age eighteen, largely to escape the clutches of my madman father, at last my mother was free.

Given my lack of direct military interests, I've often wondered if the reason God called me to help build homes for injured veterans was because I knew what it was like to survive a battlefield and then to spend the rest of my days trying my darndest to recover from the wounds I'd received. It can be childhood abuse, rape, suffering a loved one's addiction, or having to subsist below the poverty line—whatever our struggles, they mark us. I know for sure that mine marked me. And so in some ways it was completely natural that I'd gravitated toward soldiers who'd been wrecked by suffering and pain. We've got more than fifty thousand physically injured soldiers today but more than six times that amount with PTSD. The wounding is one thing, but the real test emerges as one deals with the ramifications of that wounding year after year. God must have known I was a fit sojourner for those soldiers; I had spent years in my own kind of war.

What's Mine to Do

By springtime 2006, almost exactly one year after Carol and I resolved to retire from homebuilding and adopt a more laid-back pace of life, I found myself deeply magnetized to our cause. Following completion of the Schulz family's remodel, I tried to focus intently on the projects my custom-homebuilding business had agreed to do—and given the sturdy housing market in Houston that so far seemed unfazed by the national economic crisis, there were a *bunch* of homes underway. But increasingly I had trouble focusing on anything other than building more homes for more veterans in need.

I'd done enough research by this point in time to know of the thousands of military families needing housing assistance, and the thought of them subsisting in substandard arrangements kept me up at night, unable to sleep. During those long, restless hours, I'd commit myself to prayer, asking God for clarity about what part of this mammoth problem was mine—in particular— to solve. But clear answers seemed to evade my grip, as though I had grease on my palms. Still, I knew that God had called me to this effort in the same way he called men and women in the Bible to grow their faith and follow him. Of all the biblical characters lauded in Hebrews 11 for their great faith—Abel and Enoch, Abraham and Sarah, Jacob and Joseph, Gideon and Samson, David and Samuel, and all the prophets—the one I most resonate with is Moses, the seemingly inarticulate leader of the nation Israel, who was asked to fulfill a specific role for God. In the same way that Moses was qualified for his mission only because it was God who was qualifying him, something in me knew that

God could use my life's stutter steps to walk toward an outcome that would glorify him.

Or so I believed, anyway.

Tragic Ending to a Happy Story

What I didn't know at the time was that upon wrapping up the Schulzes' remodel and diving headlong back into my "normal" job, the Schulzes themselves faced a series of terrible situations that were anything but normal. The family had loved the work we had done on the house and had high hopes for how Steven would assimilate into his new environment and, as a result, his new life. But his reentry would be bumpier than anyone could have expected—and for the father as well as the son.

Steve was having a harder time than expected accepting his son's irreversible injuries and pain. The once-strong twenty-year-old was now immobilized, barely communicative, and weak. Steven had little speech and his formerly sharp mind had become easily confused and slow. Steve, who had battled depression for much of his life, began to spiral again.

Multiplying Steve's stress was the daily care his son required. It was too much for any parent to bear, even one so deeply committed to his son. Steve's depression, anger, and sense of incompetence sent him careening deeper toward isolation and fear, and soon he became incapable of managing his thoughts, his habits, or his marriage.

I had heard rumblings about the Schulzes' struggles and tried as best I could to reach out. Soon enough, the call that I'd been dreading came: Steve had gone missing and had been gone for two weeks.

It would be six full months before Steve's body would be found, in a remote ranching area of south Texas. The family had searched the area time and again, thwarted at every turn by the thick, dense scrub brush blanketing the plains. In what would be presumed by many to be suicide, the desperate father at last was found dead.

Those who grieved the loss of Steve spanned wide and deep and far, everyone who had worked on the remodel counted among them. Why would God arrange for this family to receive such a beautiful gift, only to allow tragedy to have its way? We were heartbroken—all of us. My mind reeled as I processed the awful events. Maybe I'd gotten my wires crossed, thinking God was "calling" me to this line of work. Given the outcome of our very first endeavor, maybe this wasn't to be my path at all. I'd thought I was making life better for the Schulzes. Had I instead somehow made things worse?

For weeks following Steve's death, I pounded on the doors to heaven, asking God what I was to do. In response, he was strangely silent, as though he had nothing to add to what he'd already said. What he'd "already said" was that I was to forego retirement for a season and invest myself in serving military families in need. Those were the marching orders I'd been given, and so I decided that those were the orders I'd fulfill.

Tragic though the story was, over time, I came to see the profound honor I'd been given of seeing firsthand the gut-wrenching realities that our wounded veterans and their families face. I had been at airports for the tearful and joyous reunions of soldiers as they returned to loved ones' arms. I had been present for Memorial Day and Veterans Day gatherings, where soldiers had spoken of the privilege of service. I had watched admiringly as various military officers were honored at sporting events and prayer breakfasts and more. But never before had I been given a ringside seat to what day-to-day life for them really was like.

Knots I Couldn't Untie

While it was true that Steven Schulz had been given a handicap-accessible living area and bathroom and kitchen, and that most of his physical needs had been taken care of, the emotional and financial threads of his life were jumbled into a thousand knots, seemingly never to be untied. His mom, Debbie, had quit her job in order to shuttle Steven back and forth to the Veterans Administration hospital nearby—and then to care for his needs every hour in between. With the loss of Debbie's income and the ever-mounting expenses necessitated by Steven's situation, the numbers had become enemy, not friend.

Prior to Steven's injury, Debbie and Steve were eyeing their soon-to-be empty nest with optimism, guarded though it was. They would miss having Steven buzzing through their home day in and day out, but now that he was a grown man himself, couldn't they begin to entertain retirement, a little less responsibility and a little slowing down?

No, Debbie and Steve would need to start over now.

I'd felt a wild sense of burden on behalf of the Schulz family, and yet what on earth was I supposed to do? I was just a home-builder; I'd pretty much already done the key thing I can do. I'd rallied a bunch of friends, and together we'd made their home livable for Steven. But for some reason, I couldn't let go of this precious family.

Years prior to Steve's death, during a few minutes of prayer one morning, I was talking with God about this very situation, when he laid on my heart the idea of doing a fundraiser for the Schulzes. I thought back to when my sons Jereme and Aaron were young and would periodically participate in fundraisers for their Little League teams. They did cake auctions mostly, peddling small-town moms' home-baked goods for ten or twenty bucks a pop. The Schulz family would need more cakes than anyone could bake, but I knew I was at least on the right track. I went to my friends at BABA and explained my idea: we needed to do some sort of fundraiser to help the Schulzes get back on their feet. After a lively discussion, we landed on the idea of selling plates at a barbecue dinner and donating all proceeds to Steven and his folks.

In honor of my sons, we had done a good old-fashioned cake auction. Atop each cellophane-wrapped cake, we'd adhered a card that told the story of a family member who served in the military.

Learning one soldier's story had changed my entire life, and I was hoping that by passing along similar stories, others' lives would be similarly changed. We'd invited Texas State Representative Larry Taylor to serve as auctioneer, and as each cake was brought up for bid, he read every last one of those stories. They were tragic, as you'd expect: a fiancé who lost her soon-to-be husband, a mother who had to bury her son, a daddy's girl mourning the loss of her hero. But it was also beautiful, for in the selling of those cakes and in the passing along of those tales, more than six thousand dollars was raised for the Schulz family.

The Spirit of God had been among us in that place, evidently a fan of barbecue, cake, and the good that comes when we human types remind ourselves that we're better together than apart.

As I say, all of these efforts had certainly not been in vain. The Schulz family had been helped greatly by the acts of generosity so many in their community had done on their behalf. But in the end, the darkness that shrouded this family found a way to eclipse every last speckle of light.

To other people, the darkness may have made them question God's call on their lives and utterly run them off. But to me the whole series of events only served to secure my resolve. Military families were struggling, *deeply*, and I was dogged in my belief that in some small way I could help to relieve their pain.

Overcoming Darkness with Light

During those awful days in the wake of Steve Schulz's death, when my emotions were raw even as my faith was firm, I reflected on another life-from-death situation that God had seen fit to orchestrate in my life. Several years before Steve was laid to rest, an invitation addressed to me arrived in the mail. It was an invitation to a family reunion, sent to me courtesy of Richard Eugene Wallrath—my father.

I'd received invitations to the annual event year after year, but each time, I flung the unopened envelope into the garbage can, wanting nothing to do with the man or his events. But my heart was different that day, perhaps for the first time in a long time open to the notion of a conciliatory path. It wasn't wide open—I wouldn't say that. But there was a crack there, maybe even big enough for a little light to get through.

Later that afternoon, having noticed the letter opened and resting on my desk, Carol glanced my way and asked, "Are you thinking about going this year?" I responded, "I don't know."

It was the truth—I *didn't* know. What I did know was that if God could miraculously bring beauty from the ashes of the Schulz family's downward spiral—something I fully expected him to do—then perhaps he could raise up something beautiful in Dad and me. He and I hadn't spoken in more than twenty years. I decided that was long enough.

Leave a Legacy You Love

Spend a few minutes thinking through the following themes, based on the situations and stories from chapter 2:

1. When I was a kid, church represented safety and security to me, and still today, I find the environment extremely life-giving. What about you? Has attending church ever been part of your rhythm and routine? What images or feelings are stirred in you as you think about the concept of "church"?

2. The idea of a loving, caring heavenly Father felt foreign to me for many years, due to the abuse I suffered at my earthly father's hands. I wonder how the idea sits with you; is it natural or terribly strange to consider the thought that the God of the universe—Jehovah God—accepts you, adores you, and is committed to your wellbeing each day of your

life? What life experiences shape your thinking here?

3. What did you make of my association between my own "war" with my father as a young boy, and the empathy I feel for soldiers who return from a *real* war, wounded and in need? Have you ever considered that your struggles might actually lead you to the divine work God is calling you to do? In what ways might it be true for you?

4. My decision to attend my dad's family reunion was based in my firm belief that God really can bring beauty from ashes, a prophetic picture first offered in the Old Testament book of Isaiah, chapter 61. How does such a premise sit with you? What assumptions or firsthand experiences might be fueling your response?

3

THE BABY'S
FIRST STEPS

CHAMPION RANCH WAS the sacred object that had occupied my dad's lifelong dream. After his window business took off, taking with it Dad's chronic poverty, he purchased a series of small ranches, one after the other, still chasing that elusive dream. But in 1992, with the acquisition of a large thirty-five-hundred-acre ranch in Centerville, Texas, which Dad would augment by gobbling up another twenty-five hundred acres that flanked the space's perimeter, he'd finally hit the target. In his mind, anyway, his life was now complete.

My father's purchase of what would become Champion Ranch coincided with a failed attempt at reconciliation that he and I had made fifteen years into our estrangement, which led to the second fifteen-year estrangement we endured. And so I didn't learn firsthand about the ranch—its entry into the family, its ever-increasing number of outbuildings, its successful forays into horse and cattle breeding, and its deeply rooted charm. No, all the news I'd received came to me courtesy of my sister Pam, who was still in touch with my father regularly and would drop subtle updates here and there.

In its finished format, the ranch comprised six thousand acres of beautiful rolling hills, towering oak trees, and manicured pastures dotted with fat, happy cows as far as the eye could see. It was modeled after the world-famous King Ranch located just outside of San Antonio, in Kingsville, Texas, but my father had put his personal touches on it. Now in the summer of 2007, I'd see his pride and joy for myself.

Carol and I made the three-hour drive to Centerville, up Interstate 45, eventually entering the ranch through lofty stucco pillars reminiscent of the Old West. Upon taking in our immediate surroundings, we fell silent at the grandeur of it all. As our tires rolled slowly along the asphalt path, we scanned the immediate horizon for the myriad of structures we'd heard were there—a saloon and a bunkhouse, an office building and a working barn, an equine center and a training facility, stables and arenas, and more. It was stunning. We were so fully absorbed in the majestic setting that it took us a moment to register that a pickup truck was approaching, easing to a stop once it reached our side. The driver rolled down his window, revealing a worn, weathered face. Then, I realized I was staring into the eyes of my father. He had aged a lot since I'd last seen him, but then again, he probably thought the same of me. I reflexively smoothed my moustache, wondering if it had turned white yet, when I'd last seen the old man a decade ago.

My dad stepped down from his truck, and for a split second, I questioned my having come. What was I thinking, making this trip? Was everything going to be magically different somehow? My father was an angry man who guzzled whiskey like it was water, every single day of my young life. *That* guy was going to change? He was no more than five-foot-nine in stature, and yet he was an outright Goliath in my life.

There on the grounds of his ranch, I sat stunned as my dad climbed out of his truck and stepped purposefully toward me, his countenance gentle and his eyes a little moist. He was in his eighties now, comparatively wobbly and frail, and yet still a flash of apprehension raced through my heart: Would I say something wrong? Would I unwittingly irritate my dad? Would he raise a hand to me here and now and brand himself a monster once and for all?

In spite of history and all sorts of empirical evidence dissuading the trend, a man will always be his father's admiring son, even when that father has been a fool. And so as my dad neared, I opened my door and slid out from behind the steering wheel, awkwardly inching my way toward his frame. And then without realizing he'd reached for me, I found myself in his two-armed embrace, the top of his head reaching just below my chin. "I'm sorry," he said with a shaky voice. "I'm sorry—so sorry, Son."

In all my life, I'd never heard those words from my dad; not once had he spoken them to me. Not after the angry words, not after the whippings, not after the ostracism or isolation or distance or embarrassment or shame. He should have said them a thousand times, or maybe ten thousand times or more—they were due me at least that much. He hadn't, of course, but he'd said them now, and they were the only words I needed to hear. I softened there, in his meaningful embrace, as the needy child inside me who was desperate for his father's affection curled his lips into something of a smile. I no longer wanted to relive the past or make him pay for the wrongs he'd done. I just wanted healing, wholeness, and peace.

Maybe our feet were on the right path now.

A Rancher I Am Not

Carol and I freshened up in the bunkhouse and over the next several hours swapped hugs and smiles and stories with my cousins, aunts, uncles, and other family members I hadn't seen in eons. Being with loved ones proved therapeutic for me, as my attention was focused on something other than the numerous projects I had underway in Houston.

Throughout the afternoon, various groups of us would drive around the grounds, taking in the grazing cattle, the graceful horses, the soft creek beds, the rusty old pump jacks. It didn't take me long to see why Dad loved it out here. Being at the ranch was an instant blood-pressure regulator. The great outdoors are called great for a reason, I guess.

When the sun began her descent and several family members began saying their good-byes, my dad asked me to join him in his office alone for a few minutes. I stepped through the entrance into what seemed like a collectibles museum. There was an Old West revolver, several handsome deer mounts, belt buckles won at the Houston Livestock Show and Rodeo, photographs with notable people, and priceless books standing at attention on their shelves. As I studied the various displays, silently piecing together all the history I'd missed firsthand with my dad, he sidled up to me and without mincing words said, "Son, I want you to take over the ranch for the family."

I was floored. We hadn't so much as said hello to each other in all those years, and after a few short hours in each other's presence, he wanted to be business partners and bosom buddies? "Dad, we haven't talked in forever," I began. "How about we start with, 'How are you doing?' and go from there?"

He stared at me as though unsure of how to respond. "How is your health?" I asked, after a pause, to which he said with a hand waved through the air, "Eh. I don't want to talk about that stuff. This is a family ranch, and I want family running it."

So much about my dad looked different, but his hands . . . his hands were the same. He shoved them into the front pockets of his jeans and flicked his chin up a few inches. "What do you say? You come live here, run this place. I think you're the right fit for the job. Come do it. You'll see I'm right."

The truth was that I didn't know a lasso from a lariat; what business did I have running a ranch? By way of an explanation, though, I chose a different tack. "Dad, I have houses going up left and right in Houston right now, plus this new endeavor centered on homes for injured veterans. The grandkids are there. My life is there. I can't just drop everything and move to the ranch."

"Think about it," he said with a decisive nod of his head.

"Come on now. Let's get some grub." And with that, he was out the door.

Jeans and a Horse, If You Please

It took two years for me to pull the trigger, but once I did in the winter of 2009, practically overnight, I became a rancher. Those rolling pastures, the gentle winds that stir the tops of the pine and oak, the star-studded stars at night—sure, there are plenty of stressors inherent in running a ranch—but set against that backdrop, how bad could it be? Soon enough, I put it together that there were more similarities here to my homebuilding job than differences—swap out heifers and hay bales for sheetrock and two-by-fours, and basically I was doing the same thing. Plus, it didn't hurt that the company uniform was blue jeans and the company car was a quarter horse. Success still centered on stringent project plans, which was second nature for me, and my job still relied on a tight schedule of coordinated events, a reality that felt more like recess than work.

Carol and I kept our home in Houston because she chose to continue her work at the crisis-pregnancy center each week. She had volunteered there for more than seventeen years and felt she had been divinely called to counsel young women who were considering aborting their babies and who were desperately in need of sound advice. Neither of us wanted to see her give up such meaningful work, but our deeper motivation for our measured approach to taking over the ranch was that we were not at all convinced that my dad's change of heart was sincere. You don't undo a lifetime of painful memories with one "I'm sorry." We opted for taking things slow.

We'd give it a year, we decided, with Carol and me commuting back and forth. I'd come home every weekend so that we could keep our commitments at church, and she'd make the drive to Centerville midweek during times when her workload was light. We would ease into our new lives and assess as we went. And we'd do our level best to trust what Dad had said: that he was a new man and that our involvement at the ranch would be nothing short of a good fit.

The Writing on the Wall

A big factor in our decision to relocate to Centerville was the sudden decline in the Houston homebuilding market. For so long, the industry had held steady despite national drops, but by 2008, it was obvious the city wasn't impervious to the declines hitting everyone else. Still, this didn't automatically mean I should pick up stakes and move; after all, I'd called my south-Texas location my home base for more than thirty years. If for no other reason than for the sake of my calling on behalf of wounded vets, didn't common sense dictate that I stay put?

Upon closer scrutiny, as well as a deepened commitment to prayer, I realized that my business connections over the years had spanned far beyond those south-Texas walls. A quick mental review of my contacts revealed that my ties to nearly every other region in the country were just as strong if not stronger than my Bay Area database. What's more, it wasn't lost on me that at the very same time that my custom homebuilding efforts were missing the mark, everything I touched on behalf of in-need veterans quickly turned to gold. God was clearly up to something, and maybe a few years running, the ranch would afford me time to discover what it was.

A Needed Partner in Crime

Back in 2007, I was itching to take on a third from-the-ground-up build and was therefore elated when I was put in touch with US Marine Corps Lieutenant Erasmo Valles, a young man whose vehicle had run over an IED while serving in Iraq. A few of our BABA board members and I met him in person shortly thereafter at a hotel in League City, just outside of Houston, while he was in town, and as I watched him interact with his wife, Sandra, and their three children, I knew I was in the presence of a very special man. He had become an amputee because of the war, but his heart was still completely intact. And it was as big as Texas.

The Valleses wanted to relocate from his home base of San Antonio to Houston, Erasmo explained, so that he and Sandra could pursue their master's degrees—his in business administration and hers in teaching—at the University of Houston. But there was no money to chase such a lofty dream. They couldn't afford the relocation itself, let alone the burden of a big-city mortgage *and* higher-education fees. My mind was whirring

Erasmo Valles, First Lieutenant, US Marine Corps, and family

with ideas as I left that meeting with Erasmo and Sandra. I had a feeling we could help.

It was about this time when I decided I needed to establish the business as an official entity, as something more than just a thing I did on the side. Because my BABA colleagues had been so instrumental in the first projects, offering up supplies and services and time, a handful of them and I developed the charitable organization Bay Area Builders Association Support Our Troops (BABASOT) and set to work filing paperwork to become a bona fide 501(c)3. The name change to Operation FINALLY HOME would be an elegant and useful shift, but this would still be a few years away. For the time being, we got ourselves a dedicated checking account, even though we had no money, and we began the process of accrediting the group so that clean records of our donations and spending would always be readily available for anyone wishing to view them. The BABASOT baby was taking her first few steps, and I was as puffed chested as a first-time dad.

Simultaneous to these administrative goings-on, I was asked

to provide insight on another group's homebuilding project, underway for a soldier who had become a double amputee. With all the urgent tasks on my to-do list, I didn't have time to put out anyone else's fires. But God had planted me in this calling of helping military families, and in that moment when the request was before me, I heard myself say, "Sure. I'll come."

In God's typical mind-blowing style, that singular meeting during which I thought I was offering up a favor to someone I barely knew proved to be a real turning point for my own business. It was a blessing I sorely needed, and it was laid right in my lap.

Unbeknownst to me, an operations whiz named Daniel Vargas had also been invited to the meeting. He was working with a different nonprofit at the time, and as the meeting kicked off, he looked at me and said, "So, Dan, what exactly is your role within your organization, BABASOT?"

"I'm not entirely sure," I said with a grin. "I came into this whole deal as a builder, but here lately I've served as a marriage counselor, a banker, a lawyer, a chief negotiator, and, just last week, a babysitter." I ticked off the jobs one by one on my fingers and then opened my hand wide with a shrug, as if to say, "And who knows what next week will bring?"

Daniel Vargas was unfazed. Nodding, he said, "Yep. Been there, done that too." We shared a laugh, and instantly, I knew I'd found a friend.

Throughout the meeting, I caught snippets of Daniel's story. And I grew more and more impressed with him as he shared. He was in the US Air Force and had served both in Desert Storm and Desert Shield. A couple of years prior, he was still on active duty serving at Randolph Air Force Base in San Antonio, Texas, and was in and out of Brooke Army Medical Center there, in order to have his various medical issues treated. He wanted more than anything to be redeployed to Iraq, but he'd been informed he was considered undeployable for health reasons. For him, the next best thing to being side-by-side with his servicemen and servicewomen was supporting them there at the hospital, hearing their stories and serving their needs. Brooke Army Medical Center was where burn victims and amputee patients were sent; there would be *plenty* of stories to hear and plenty of needs to meet.

Daniel told me that during his first few days roaming the halls at Brooke, he made a habit of asking recovering soldiers what they did for fun. Most of them thought the question was ludicrous, given their compromised position: "Nothing," they answered. "This place isn't really designed for 'fun.'"

Daniel decided to take matters into his own hands, beginning with securing free tickets and backstage passes to an upcoming Toby Keith concert in town. He had to jump through a series of hoops, but eventually, he had obtained the tickets—and also permission from the hospital to release ten patients for a few hours—and the group of injured vets was on its way. From there, he established connections with other musical headliners and a variety of sports teams. Ten or twelve patients at a time, he'd treat those recovering veterans to a fun-filled evening free of therapy and medical tests. On occasion, when donations failed to fully cover incidentals, Daniel would even dig into his own pocket to fund a rental van or gas. "It was worth it every time," he told me, "just to see those guys have a good time."

On the professional front, Daniel explained to me that the organization he was working with had expertise in fundraising, but that they struggled on the building front. Of course the opposite was true for me. My pals and I knew building like the back of our hands but were still coming up quite a learning curve regarding securing donations and keeping financially afloat. Before we'd parted ways that day, I locked eyes with

Daniel Vargas and Dan

him and said, "Listen, we can build the homes, if you can help us raise the money." Then and there, a deal was sealed.

The next day, Daniel began reaching out to his contacts to explain our newfound collaboration. Within hours, he and his network had secured the necessary funding to purchase the Valles lot. What I couldn't have known yet was that the expert effectiveness and efficiency I'd witnessed from Daniel in that first endeavor was just how the guy rolled. He is a pro, through and through.

Soon enough, Daniel noticed the vast potential of BABASOT and also the wild lack of funding we possessed toward realizing it. "We need to do a fundraiser," he suggested. "A real one. Something big." The ensuing explanation flowed easily from his lips. We'd put on a charity concert, with proceeds going to BABASOT. It would be held in a world-class arena, it would feature world-class talent, and it would rake in some serious coin. Within a matter of days, Daniel had booked the Pasadena Rodeo Association's facility; he had overseen the selection of a name—"Bands for Brothers and Sisters"—as well as the design for a logo (a soldier with a guitar on his back), which would be pressed onto t-shirts, bumper stickers, coins, and badges; he had confirmed an impressive list of

Bands for Brothers and Sisters Concert in Pasadena, TX (poster)

Bands for Brothers and Sisters Concert, featuring Ted Nugent

entertainers and a well-known emcee; and he had solidified his place in my mind as an invaluable addition to my team.

Everyone whom Daniel had invited to participate was willing to perform at a significantly cut rate, which helped our margins tremendously and made the financial aspect of the event a breeze. But there were still the logistics and mechanics of pulling off a live concert to contend with. Neither Daniel nor I had ever managed artists, lighting and sound considerations, ticket sales, or security. It was a massive undertaking for us, but with Daniel at my side, I honestly believed anything was possible. It didn't shock me in the least when the night went off without a hitch. As the concert ended, I looked at Daniel and said, "We need to go national, my friend."

I didn't want to get ahead of ourselves, but something in me knew there was more than the euphoria of our immediate success driving my remark. Daniel Vargas was a God-given gift in my life, and I didn't want to let him get away.

As time went on, Daniel and I only grew more comfortable in our working relationship. We often talked about how God was leading us to invest more of our time and talent into serving our country's war-wounded folks and how we believed we had stumbled upon a unique partnership the day our paths crossed. For a time, it had worked fine for us to join forces under a collaborative umbrella, me still working from the BABASOT side and him still working from his organization's side. But the deeper our collaboration grew, the more our unified vision eclipsed everything. We needed to work together—on the same team headed in the same direction, both of us all-in. I needed to hire Daniel and make him my first official employee, and I needed to do it now. And so I picked up the phone to make a call to my friend, opening with, "Brother, I've got good news, and I've got bad news. Which of the two do you want first?"

Good News, Bad News

The good news was that I wanted to hire Daniel; the bad was that I didn't have any money to pay him. It says everything you need to know about the man that his reaction to my quandary was hearty laughter. "Are you serious?" he asked, to which I said, "Totally. But God has provided for us up until this point, and I'm sure he will provide from here on out. What do you need to bring in, in order to make this thing worth your while?"

Daniel told me the salary he was currently making, even though he knew I couldn't come close to matching it. "Well, this is where it helps that you're a master fundraiser," I said with a laugh. "Your first task as BABASOT's first employee is to go raise money for your paycheck."

Behind our joking around was a set of serious issues. Daniel was going through a divorce and had full custody of the couple's only child, a daughter named Raini. He was fighting to keep his home, which doubled as his office, and desperately needed steady income, given all the tumult in his life. His current organization could provide continuity, even as his heart wanted to jump on board with me. This matter would require deep devotion to prayer, which is exactly what we both gave it. When Daniel eventually called with the news that he was joining BABASOT formally, I knew it was a God-ordained deal.

"I do have one condition," Daniel explained, before we ended our call that day. "As soon as our projects no longer center on loving families and helping them to thrive, I'm out." To which I replied, "Deal. You got yourself a deal."

In September of 2009, Daniel became the first employee of Bay Area Builders Association Support our Troops. He worked from his home office in New Braunfels, Texas, just a few hours from Houston, and also the seat of our firm's new home base. One of Daniel's passions, besides the nonprofit side, was helping soldiers' families navigate the choppy waters of postmilitary life, including working with insurance companies; seeking out necessary medical services; and seizing opportunities for advanced schooling, career placement, and military retirement.

Additionally, word quickly circulated that Daniel and BABA-SOT refused to employ the typical sterile application process used by most charitable organizations, instead opting for engaging in robust interviews with prospective recipients, which meant an influx of interested partners, providers, and families in need came our way.

By the end of that year, we had completed four projects in the Houston area, we had established legitimate sources of income, and we were still burning brightly with passion to help more families as God saw fit. Which is perhaps why Daniel thought it an appropriate step to take to submit my name to CNN for consideration as one of that year's "heroes." My associate could see what was also becoming clear to me, that this BABASOT baby, while a little wobbly at first, was finally walking, sure and strong.

Leave a Legacy You Love

Spend a few minutes thinking through the following themes, based on the situations and stories from chapter 3:

1. Seeing my dad at the ranch for that family reunion represented a defining moment for me, one that infused my cynicism with vast amounts of hope and gave me a vision for the future I believed I was supposed to pursue. As you reflect on your own journey, what are some of your defining moments when you sensed a real change of direction from something harmful to something helpful or from isolation to a coming together again?

2. The entrance of Daniel Vargas into my story was an undeniable gift from God. Looking back on the "defining moment" seasons you've been part of, who did God allow to join you on the path? What role did that person (or those

people) play? What benefits did you receive as a result of their sojourning with you?

3. As you ponder the God-given calling before you, who in your life today might be divinely placed sojourners, people who can lend energy and encouragement to your days?

4

GETTING GOOD
AT THE ASK

THERE'S A CURIOUS injunction in the Bible that goes like this: "Ask, and it will be given to you; seek, and you will find; knock, and it will be opened to you. For everyone who asks receives, and he who seeks finds, and to him who knocks it will be opened" (Matthew 7:7-8). I didn't fully understand this litany of promises when I first turned over my life to God, but I would soon discover that he absolutely meant what he said. Just a year or two into our marriage, Carol discovered a lump on her breast—news that sent me reeling as I catastrophized, fretted, and groaned. I was all of nineteen years old and had staked 100 percent of my livelihood on this wonderful woman. What if cancer was found? What if she died? I cringed as I waited for those test results, unsure I could go on at all without her at my side.

Somewhere in that mix of sleepless nights and wringing of hands, though, I thought about that passage in Matthew 7, and I decided to give it a try. I'd heard Carol's dad, our pastor James Prince, offer up powerful prayers from the pulpit each weekend, and while I was no match for his eloquence, I fumbled my way through my own version of a prayer, asking God in nearly incomprehensible fashion to please not let my wife die. I prayed for good test results. I prayed for the "C" word not to come into play. I prayed the whole deal would miraculously go away and that we would be able to happily continue building our lives. I didn't know exactly what to ask God for, but ask and ask I did. And wouldn't you know it: within a week we learned that nothing was going to come of it. Carol was fine; I was fine; and life was fine.

It was an early lesson for me in taking God at his word, a lesson that decades later would serve as the hinges on which the door of my business swung. Indeed, if it is a good and godly thing to "ask" for whatever we wish, then boy did I get good and godly in the early days of Operation FINALLY HOME.

Life Outside My Comfort Zone

It never has been easy for me to ask people for things. Resources were so slim when I was growing up that it would never occur to me to ask my parents or anyone else for whatever it was I wanted; my dad was so prideful and self-sufficient that he never once modeled the humility required to ask another person for anything; and by all accounts, given my lack of formal education, the explanation for how I later became a business owner was that I knew how to make my own way in the world. But now my success hinged on rallying scores of people to a shared cause. I had no other option but to ask—for buildable lots; for supplies; for labor; for cold, hard cash. Interestingly, over time the asking part got easier, largely because my passion for the projects was just that high.

During our build for Melanie and Chris LeBleu, the marine who contracted the deadly virus while serving in Iraq, I met Peter Sutton, who also was a marine who had served in Iraq.[1] And just like Blue, he had a harrowing tale to tell. He'd had one of his legs nearly blown off, and while the VA staff was doing everything they could do to save the limb, the outlook was bleak. To make matters worse, Peter and his wife, Caroline, were walking through a season of high stress. He was retiring from the military because of his injuries, and she was pregnant and very sick, making employment a nonoption for them both. I knew I had to help these folks.

The couple and their three young girls were living with Caroline's parents, but even without housing costs temporarily, it was a tight squeeze. What's more, Peter was wrestling with symptoms of PTSD, a condition that, over time, I learned plagued nearly every marine, army soldier, air force airman, and navy seaman. Triggers could include the most ordinary noises: the goings-on at a construction site, a car backfiring, a door slamming in the wind. Reflexively, the trigger would transport the war veteran back to the battlefield—and to the concussion of bombs, automatic gunfire, and overwhelming chaos that went with it. The sufferer could fall into something of a daze until the memory passed, or else could erupt, lashing out at whomever happened to be near. For Peter, it was always important to have a quiet room to go to when he was episodic, a place where he could retreat from the bustle and noise.

For those of us assessing the Suttons' situation, building them a home seemed like an obvious way that we could provide them much-needed relief. We would surprise them with the news at a BABA luncheon, an occasion that wound up making me feel like the Texas version of Santa Claus. It really is better to give than to receive, and the elation written on the faces of Peter and Caroline lifted the group's collective spirits to the highest height. But with the moment behind us, the real work had to begin, and just like before, nothing was going to get done without the massive efforts of a lot of people besides me. I knew it was time to make some asks.

I started with my younger son, Aaron. He and his brother, Jereme, both have the homebuilding gene, and given the fact that Aaron had already been building homes with me, he was a perfect candidate for this project. He also had a huge heart for helping others; I knew he'd love to pitch in. Upon receiving his enthusiastic yes, I named him a colead builder, the one who would be at my side throughout the build. Next, we needed to secure a buildable lot. We had pinpointed a new development in League City, south of Houston, called Tuscan Lakes. The community's owner, Larry

Johnson, was a high-powered businessman who really knew his stuff. He agreed to meet with me, and as I entered his impressive downtown-Houston office to discuss my need, I reiterated to God my complete dependence on him. "Regardless of how this meeting goes," I prayed, "I trust you fully to provide."

After Larry and I exchanged pleasantries, I explained our work, citing the LeBleu family as a recent success story. I told him that another family—the Suttons—needed our help, and that my team and I wanted to build them a mortgage-free custom home right inside one of his developments, Tuscan Lakes.

Larry was immediately interested in our proposal. "How much money have you raised so far?" he asked, a question that made my stomach do a flip. Despite my inner turmoil, I mustered the confidence to answer honestly: "None, Larry. None."

Same Song, Next Verse

I was beginning to sound like a broken record: "Yes, I am serious. Yes, I need your help. No, I can't pay whatever amount you're about to require." Thankfully, the power of our cause always saved the day. The reality was that sick and injured soldiers were returning from war to family members who would then have to unexpectedly quit their jobs in order to become caregivers for their loved ones, and given the loss of that person's paycheck and the gaps in military insurance coverage, this dynamic all but guaranteed financial devastation.

The LeBleu family had been a perfect illustration of this, and one that was heavy on my heart as I talked with Larry Johnson about the Sutton build. When I'd first met Chris LeBleu—"Blue"—I couldn't help but notice the sickly yellow shade of his skin. I would quickly learn that his condition was so critical that he had to be treated not at the VA but at the Houston Medical Center. Melanie resigned from her work so that she could drive her husband to his daily doctor appointments, and without her paychecks, the couple was down to $1,200 per month in income,

$1,100 of which went to paying their rent. Their request of our group was for a new couch that Chris could recline comfortably on. They had no idea we were also going to give them a house to put that couch in.

Our team knew that the LeBleus' lot would need to be in close proximity to the Medical Center, which happened to be near Rice University and Houston's museum district—not exactly a part of town known for inexpensive housing. As I weighed this particular dilemma, God put a name in my mind—Bud Goza, a deacon at our church and also, handily, a land developer. The following Sunday, I approached Bud and asked him if he had a lot in a bedroom community near the main artery that leads into the Medical Center, to which Bud, in his eternally easygoing manner, laughed and asked, "Why in the world would you need a lot down there?"

I explained to Bud what our vision was for the LeBleus. Immediately, his wheels were turning. "I've got the perfect spot," Bud said. "How much money you got?"

Returning Bud's smile, I said, "Nothing." I added that I'd be willing to raise whatever funds he deemed necessary in order to consider the transaction a fair value and then told him we could touch base by phone after he'd had a chance to connect with his associates. I had no idea what to expect following that impromptu hallway meeting, but I was certain about our cause, and I was certain God would provide.

Within a matter of days, I was speeding down the highway en route to meet Bud at a lot. I hopped out of my truck, shook Bud's hand, and took in the land on which we stood. "You were

Chris Lebleu, Lance Corporal, US Marine Corps, and Melanie Lebleu

right, Bud," I said with a grin. "This place is exactly the spot." A lot is typically nothing more than a piece of inventory, but this plot of land was different. It would be for the LeBleus true hope. Bud and I bid each other farewell that day, still without having discussed the matter of price.

The following Sunday, I sidled up to Bud and said, "Well, Bud, have you sorted out the price?"

Of course he smiled. "Well, Dan, how much have you raised?"

"None, my friend," I said. "Haven't yet raised a cent."

To which Bud said, as he looked me square in the face, "I think I'll just give you that lot."

You could have knocked me over with a feather. A piece of prime real estate . . . for *free?* I wanted to bear-hug that old man. "God is still in the business of working miracles!" I said. I shouldn't have been the least bit surprised.

The LeBleu build had come together in a matter of nine months, an eighteen-hundred-square-foot home with as many bells and whistles as the fanciest mansion. It was a beauty. The scores of generous suppliers who had said yes to my ask provided not leftover stock but their very best—and it showed. Handmade wood cabinets, granite countertops, tile and wood flooring, custom showers and tubs, intricate crown molding, expensive knobs and pulls on kitchen and bathroom cabinets and drawers—this place had it all. And then to top it off, I made sure to get that new couch. I placed a call to Gallery Furniture, owned by a man who called himself Mattress Mac, and explained to him the LeBleus' situation. "What do they need?" Mac asked me, to which I answered, "A new couch. Plus everything else."

On the day we handed over the keys to Chris and Melanie outside their new home, a huge Gallery Furniture truck pulled up to the curb, loaded to its rims with a house full of new furniture.

Nothing about the project made sense. A picturesque lot in a desirable neighborhood for free? A $200,000 home built for less than six grand in donated funds? An entire house full of new furniture at no cost to the owners of that home? "You gotta be *kidding* me," I said to God with a shake of my head and a laugh. I imagined him laughing right back.

Praying for Another Yes

Back in Larry Johnson's office, I couldn't help but flash back to the LeBleu build, subconsciously telegraphing to Larry the word *yes*. I knew if he agreed to help us on behalf of the Sutton family, he'd never once regret that choice. And yet this was no grandfatherly deacon I was dealing with; Larry was a real-deal developer who had a serious business to run. In response to my honest answer about having no money to offer him for the lot, he said he would huddle with the others at Johnson Development and get back to me. As I left the building, emerging into blazing Houston heat, I reminded myself of what I'd just asked for. The price of a lot in Tuscan Lakes, just the pad of dirt alone, was valued at approximately $40,000—a big ask, to be sure.

In the end, we got that lot for free, thanks to Larry's and his team's generosity and care. "My group was moved by the plight of our soldiers," Larry explained later. "We had to be part of the team."

Similar to the LeBleu project, Peter and Caroline's build was completed in nine months' time, a home worth more than $260,000 built for just under twenty-five grand. And the whole thing was done without my even possessing a checkbook. In two words: *only God*.

Asks of a Different Sort

Peter, Caroline, and their three daughters moved into their new home and enthusiastically began a fresh chapter in their life as homeowners. At last, a place they could call their own. Peter was still very involved in his rehabilitation and seemed to be doing well, but about six months after they'd moved into their home, I received a frantic call. It was Caroline on the other end, and she was sobbing uncontrollably, barely able to talk. She was hiding in her closet, she sputtered out in whispered syllables, while her husband raged outside. Peter was having a PTSD episode when he tried to choke Caroline. She begged me to come and help.

During the quick five-mile drive to the Suttons' house, I prayed for insight, and for peace. Was I going to have to wrestle a marine? I felt sure I knew who would win, and while I'm no slouch, it wouldn't be me. Did Peter own any weapons? Probably, he did. Was he still in an angry rage? If so, what was I going to do? Were his daughters in danger as well? They shouldn't see their daddy like this. So many questions, so few answers, and so little time to waste. I pulled into Peter's driveway and threw my truck into park. With no plan in place and no defense save for prayer, I began to beat on the front door while hollering Peter's name.

Eventually, Peter opened the door looking enraged, psychotic, and mean. He was staring at me—through me, actually—and before he could utter a syllable or make a move of his own, I reached out, grabbed him by the collar, dragged him outside, and began to verbally rip him up one side and down the other. "We did not build a home for you so that you would treat your family like this!" I screamed at the top of my lungs. "You will not treat your wife this way!"

I berated him for what felt like half an hour before I observed him starting to melt. The man could have beaten me to a pulp in those moments, but for whatever reason, he didn't. I remain grateful for that little fact.

When I saw that Peter's expression had shifted from rage to shame, I told him to get into my truck. I rushed inside the house to check on Caroline and the girls, who all were still crying and visibly shaken. It appeared they were fine physically, and so I hugged Caroline and assured her that Peter was himself again and that he and I would return after taking a drive. I wanted to be sure he was calm enough to reengage with his family, and that there would be no further incidents that night.

After climbing back into my truck, I told Peter how disappointed I was that he had harmed Caroline so deeply—physically, verbally, and emotionally. I'd probably sounded like a lunatic out there on his front lawn, hollering about the fact that I didn't build homes for bullies. But my motivation was pure: when my team and I select a family to build for, we are inviting them into *our* family, and one of our family's house rules is that we represent the organization well. Suddenly, one apology after the next began to tumble from Peter's lips. Rage wasn't in his nature, he said. He couldn't for the life of him understand why he'd snapped.

Peter and I drove around the city for an hour before making our way back to his house. On the way back, I stopped by a local floral shop, handed Peter two twenties, and said, "Go get something nice for Caroline." A flower arrangement wasn't going to fix the pain they both felt, but maybe it would ease his reentry some. Minutes later, a hunched-over Peter rang the doorbell to his own home and upon seeing his wife fell into her waiting arms. He apologized through tears, she hugged him through tears, and I stood as an outside observer, shedding a few tears of my own. I hugged them both and departed, struck with fresh awareness of how much my recipient families mean to me.

It would be months later that I would learn the right way to help a soldier through a PTSD episode, a calming and controlled protocol devoid of yelling, shaming, and berating. (Oops.) It was knowledge I would file away as an answer to prayer, one that sounded like a different sort of ask: "Father, would you show me how to care for these families I'm building homes for? I don't want to be just their homebuilder; I also want to be their friend. And yet these issues they're facing are so massive. Lord God, what's mine to do?"

Chris LeBleu had faced massive issues as well. He had taken possession of his new home with his amazing wife, Melanie, and they were prepared for a wonderful life ahead, including bike rides, lots of laughter, maybe a child or two, Little League, the whole bit. But none of that was to be. Over the weeks and months after they moved in, Chris' health deteriorated. He'd received a liver transplant, and while their new home afforded them easy access to Houston Medical Center for treatments and checkups, in short order his liver began to fail. Soon thereafter, Chris died.

I remember having long, hard conversations with God over that turn of events. *Why* was a frequent question I asked, and the response I heard each and every time was this: "You keep doing what I've asked you to do, and I'll keep supplying the resources to do it. I will help you overcome every obstacle you face, including the emotional ones, like this."

God was proving true to his word; even on the heels of Chris' death, I felt strangely at peace.

At Chris' funeral, Melanie called me aside and asked what she should do with her home. I think she assumed that because her Marine Corps husband had passed away, the one for whom the house ostensibly was built, she ought to give it up, maybe pass it along to another injured veteran so that he or she could be blessed in the same way that Melanie and Chris had been blessed. While I was touched by her generosity, I knew I had to halt her train of thought immediately. "It's *your* home, Melanie," I said. "Free and clear. Forever. We can never repay you for the sacrifice your family has made on our country's behalf. That home is the very least any of us can do."

With tears in her eyes, she simply said thanks.

Good Messy

By the end of 2008, I had invested three years in the calling God had given me without really stopping to think how I was being changed along the way. Losing Chris forced me to evaluate why the hit had hurt so badly. The truth was that through the process of building homes for survivors of war, my own survivor heart was being knitted to each of theirs. I loved the men and women and children I was creating housing for. I loved them like I love my own kids. And so every challenge they faced, every battle they were asked to fight, every issue they had to resolve became, on some level, my challenges, my battles, my issues to take on. I don't mean we forged codependent strongholds—not at all. It's just that what I thought would be a professional endeavor at the outset wound up being personally gratifying in a way that's tough to put words to. Yes, it was often messy—dealing with pain and brokenness (physical as well as emotional) always is. But I would call it good-messy. Messy that has purpose. Messy that makes us better in the end.

There's an age-old military mantra that says, "Service before self," and every single recipient of the homes I was building seemed to live each day by that code. The selflessness had a way of rubbing off on me, and a few short years into the process, I could see that God was using those banged-up vets to round off some of the hard edges I'd been carrying around for years. It made me wonder if that wasn't my heavenly Father's grand scheme in this whole deal—not the homebuilding but the rebuilding of me. Either way, I could tell that the vision he had given me was coming to fruition, and truth be told, I hadn't seen *anything* yet.

Leave a Legacy You Love

Spend a few minutes thinking through the following themes, based on the situations and stories from chapter 4:

1. I mentioned at the beginning of this chapter my captivation with the promise of Matthew 7:7-8, which says that if we ask, we will receive what we've asked for; if we seek, we will find; and if we knock, the door will be opened for us. As it relates to finding a fulfilling mission for your life—your "calling"—what things do you want to ask God for today? Do you need greater clarity? More time or money or energy?

Answers to questions? Physical or emotional healing? The camaraderie of one true friend? Wisdom, perspective, or hope? I wonder how you'd answer that question. I wonder what you'd ask God for.

2. For me, there emerged a direct correlation between my willingness to bring my heartfelt requests to God, and the "uncanny" way I'd then encounter living, breathing people down here on earth who were eager to meet my needs. Coincidence? I highly doubt it. This was God—at his finest—at work. What about you? Do you tend to trust God with the daily needs you face or insist on going it alone? What might happen if you come to your heavenly Father this week first and then see what unfolds from there?

3. Along the way, I felt like God conveyed to me, *You keep doing what I've asked you to do, and I'll keep supplying you the resources to do it. I will help you overcome every obstacle you face, including the emotional ones.* Have you ever sensed this type of reassurance from your heavenly Father? If so, what were the circumstances involved? If not, may I invite you to receive it now? Read the passage below, inserting your name in the blanks you find there.

For the Lord your God is living among _____.
   He is a mighty savior.
He will take delight in _____ with gladness.
   With his love, he will calm all _____'s fears.
   He will rejoice over _____ with joyful songs."
"I will gather you who mourn for the appointed festivals;
_____ will be disgraced no more.

And I will deal severely with all who have oppressed
_____.

I will save the weak and helpless ones;
I will bring together those who were chased away.
I will give glory and fame to my former exiles,
    wherever they have been mocked and shamed.
On that day I will gather you together
    and bring _____ home again.
I will give _____ a good name, a name of distinc-
tion, among all the nations of the earth,
as I restore _____ fortunes before their very eyes.
    I, the Lord, have spoken!"
(Zephaniah 3:17-20, NLT)

5

GOING BIG-TIME

WHEN I STARTED my homebuilding business in my twenties, one of the first friends I made was Lee Kirgan, a man my same age who owned the local lumberyard. During our early conversations, I remember thinking, *This is a man I want to be friends with.* There was instant chemistry between us; he had that "loyal" look about him, and I had a feeling he and I would be comrades for a very, very long time. Given that four decades later I still count him one of my closest friends, my initial hunches were dead on. Lee is Old Faithful. He's been incredibly faithful to me.

In early 2009, Lee and I visited on several occasions about how to further Operation FINALLY HOME efforts on behalf of wounded soldiers. He and I both knew that unlocking our access to builder associations in other regions of the country would most quickly and most efficiently enable us to expand our work nationwide. But how could we reach them? The last thing I wanted to do was spend all my time and money hopping planes across the nation in order to tell one organization at a time about our vision and mission and values, and while I was getting better at making big asks, I wasn't exactly seeking out opportunities to do so. He and I agreed each time to commit the matter to prayer and then got busy doing the work that was in front of us.

Except that that's not all Lee did. Yes, he prayed. And yes, he proved faithful to show up with connections and real skills each and every time we launched a new build. But behind the scenes, he also sent an e-mail to the National Association of Homebuilders (NAHB) regarding their upcoming convention to be held in Las Vegas. The annual gathering, known as the NAHB International Builders' Show, or IBS, is to those in the homebuilding industry what the Super Bowl is to pro football players. Everybody wanted to be there, and everybody who was anybody was. More than fifty thousand builders, suppliers, bankers, and developers from around the world flocked to the convention center, searching out connections, materials, and business strategies that would take their work to the next level. It would have been a great event for my ragtag and I to attend, but the commitment wasn't cheap. Enter Lee's e-mail.

"Would you consider allowing a booth for a nonprofit?" Lee inquired, which probably made the NAHB recipient fall apart in waves of laughter. Booths for the trade show portion of the convention sell out a year in advance and cost thousands of dollars to secure. Thousands of dollars we certainly didn't have. There was no way they were going to grant that request—or so I thought.

Several days after Lee hit Send on his note, he received a reply. "We have heard about the fine work you and your group have been doing in the Houston area, and we would be honored to have you attend IBS. We have reserved a booth for you, free of charge."

Huh?

This was unheard of in the industry. It's probably unheard of in any industry. It felt too good to be true.

Viva Las Vegas!

Shortly after my small group of my colleagues and I touched down in Nevada, we were briefed on how the opening session of the convention would unfold, which was scheduled for the following day. The show was centered on a patriotic theme (what were the chances?) and would include several emotional stories of brave men and women who had served and, in some cases, died for our country's freedom. There would be elaborate backdrops, singers, dance numbers, fancy lighting tricks, and all the Vegas bells and whistles attendees had come to expect. "For your part," our host then explained, "we'd like for you, Dan, to come onstage and make a five- to seven-minute speech that introduces everyone to your organization and the work you've been doing down in Texas."

Instinctively, my palms beaded up with sweat. *A speech? Me? Here?*

"You want me to talk to the whole gathering?" I said, to which he confirmed that yes, indeed, he did. "Is that a problem?" he asked.

In fact, this was a big, big problem. Up to that point, I'd only ever spoken at our tiny BABA group's board meetings or at my church, also a small group, to present a piddly report. I wasn't prepared for anything of this sort, and although our host went on with his comments, I didn't hear another word he said.

As we were leaving the convention hall, I pulled an NAHB representative aside and asked, "Do I have this right? Our host seemed to indicate to my team and I that the entire opening ceremony speech is going to revolve around our work."

"Yes, yes! You've got it right," he said, a little too enthusiastically. More beads of sweat. More waves of terror.

"With everything going on overseas," he continued, "we thought that BABASOT was the absolute perfect example of what the homebuilding industry is all about—putting together quality products for people needing a place to call home."

I tried to reflect his optimism, even as I thought I might throw up. "God, you're going to have to show up and work a miracle, if I'm going to get through this situation alive," I prayed quietly, as I made my way to the rental car. While it's true that failure stretches a person's faith, I was living proof that success can stretch it even more.

Peace That Surpasses Understanding

The next morning dawned, and I felt as unsure as I had that first day. My group made our way to the convention hall and quickly was ushered backstage, where I was face-powdered and producer-prompted for my portion of the show. Mere moments before the emcee was supposed to call my name, inviting me to take the stage and deliver my prepared speech, the stagehand looked at me and said, "Hey, man, you all right? You look like you might pass out."

The guy was more discerning than he knew. My knees were weak, my hands wouldn't quit shaking, and I was pouring sweat from nearly every pore on my body. I took a deep breath, mustered a smile, and said to the stagehand, "Let's get this thing done."

The curtain opened, I took my first steps into the flood of stage lights, and I kid you not: a supernatural peace descended on me that I had never known before and have not experienced at that level again since. It felt as though someone had given me a shot of adrenaline, and the confidence that coursed through my veins was impossible to hide. I was energized for the task at hand and remember thinking, as I took in the packed house in front of me, *This is a blast.*

International Builders' Show in Las Vegas

At the conclusion of my remarks, the crowd jumped to their feet in a standing ovation. "That's for you, God, you see?" I whispered. "You deserve every bit of this applause."

Just before I left the stage, I encouraged the crowd to join me in helping our nation's heroes. "If you're interested," I said on a whim, "stop by our booth later on. I'd love to shake your hand."

The opening ceremony came to a close, and my team and I rose to head toward the exhibit hall, where our reserved booth was located. As we snaked our way through the throng of people, I replayed the morning's events. All that anxiety, all that fear, all that inner turmoil regarding giving a five-minute speech, and then *poof!* As profoundly as I'd experienced those emotions, in a singular moment, they were gone. In my own defense, the reason I'd been so angst ridden over the whole deal was that I was relatively new to this type of work—managing a nonprofit, working on behalf of veterans, rallying others to a cause instead of being in control and going it alone. Mostly, I hadn't wanted to screw up. I knew the stakes were high, and I desperately wanted to get it right.

What the stagehand rightly observed in my disposition was that I really was about to pass out, and yet at that pivotal moment, when it was do or die, my heavenly Father steadied my stance, lifted my chin, and proved that with him all things are possible. I thanked him silently for his provision as I rounded the corner to our exhibit area, which is when I caught sight of the line a country mile long leading into our booth. Builders and suppliers from almost every state wanted to know what they could do, how they could get involved, when they could start to help. For the balance of that convention—three very full days—my team and I spoke individually with hundreds of folks about our program and the part they could play.

What an answer to prayer it all was. I'm glad I didn't faint away; it would have been a shame to miss it all.

Better Than Good

Following the excitement at the builders' show, good news continued to roll in, again courtesy of my amazing friend Lee. Months prior, it was Lee who hatched the idea to apply for a grant with Newman's Own Foundation, a collaboration between famed actor Paul Newman and his friend A. E. Hotchner. The duo had launched a line of salad dressings in the early 1980s that attracted massive market attention. In response to the unexpected success, Newman said simply, "Let's just give it all away." And since 1982, they have: almost every penny of profit earned from Newman's Own products—which now include pizza, pasta, popcorn, lemonade, cookies, candies, coffee, even dog food—goes to people in need. Which would include, to my astonishment, *us*.

On the heels of IBS, Lee was informed that we had not only won the grant but that the folks from the foundation wanted us to be part of an awards presentation at the Pentagon in Washington, DC A few short weeks later, Lee, Daniel, and I boarded a jet bound for our nation's capital. I was smiling from ear to ear. What was God going to do next?

The next two days were a blur of activity, including meeting a four-star general, observing firsthand a retiring-of-the-flag ceremony, visiting the Hall of Heroes inside the Pentagon, and shaking hands with the Chairman of the Joint Chiefs of Staff. I was thanked for the work my team was doing and told that our efforts were filling a crucial gap between what our wounded veterans need upon returning from a tour of service and what our government can actually do. The flight home gave me space to see with fresh eyes just how valuable my God-given calling was.

Around the same time, Daniel reached out to the oil-industry group North American Petroleum and Engineering (NAPE) that met biannually in Houston to discuss industry trends and to make contributions to charitable organizations. Daniel had caught wind that the group wished to make a donation to a military nonprofit that year, and as a result of his efforts, our team was awarded the prize. We had no idea what their donation would look like as we headed to the recognition luncheon that same month—even a gift of a few hundred dollars would go a long way with us. You can imagine our shock, then, when the giant mock check symbolizing a real check was handed over, and it read, "$25,000.00." It was largest single donation we'd ever received, only to be topped by the NAPE gathering exactly one year later, when they gifted us with fifty grand.

There is a Bible verse in Psalm 81 that says of God, "open your mouth wide, and I will fill it," and that's exactly how I would characterize my experience as I set foot into 2010. God was keeping his word that he would provide every last thing I needed, in order to fulfill the mission he'd asked me to accept. As thoughts of gratitude flooded my mind for the umpteenth time in a matter of a few short years, I received a call from the producer with CNN who informed me that my name had been chosen along with twenty-four others, and I was officially a top-twenty-five contender for the CNN *Heroes* award. I never dreamed it would progress beyond that wonderful accomplishment, but alas, as spring gave way to summer and summer came to a close, I received the phone call that would change everything for me, the one informing me that I had made the top ten.

Carol was with me when I heard the big news, and as I hung up the phone, she smiled and said, "I guess Daniel knew what he was talking about after all." The "Daniel" she was referring to was Daniel Vargas, the culprit who had gone behind my back and submitted my application to CNN months prior. I shook my head with a grin and said, "Vargas. Crazy man." The truth was that I never would have been able to keep things afloat without Daniel's infectious optimism, his undying devotion to our mission, and his deep-rooted faith in God. He was a friend who'd become like a brother. He was God's gift to me—that I was sure.

A Wild, Wonderful Whirlwind

CNN requested a slew of phone calls with me over the ensuing days, as well as access to my calendar so they could trail me with a camera crew and capture exactly the type of work we were up to. We had two builds underway, and their producers and camera operators zigged when we zigged and zagged when we zagged. It was a strange sensation to know that every syllable I uttered was being recorded, but when I considered the potential end game in it all—that this endeavor God had handed me could be recognized on a national scale—my heart nearly burst with pride.

The CNN crews—both video and photographic—and my team filmed from morning until night for several days straight, and the experience taught me two definitive lessons: first, it takes nearly six thousand camera snaps to yield about three usable photographs; and second, "being on TV" isn't nearly as glamorous as I imagined it would be. Scenes had to be reshot more times than I could count. Angles and lighting had to be just so. Segments had to be reviewed and approved and redone if approval didn't come through. It was annoying, to say the least. But that carrot at the end of the stick kept me going through it all: if the rigmarole would somehow lead to more people knowing about the plight our good soldiers faced, then I would have stayed out there mugging for cameras for twenty-four hours a day, one hundred days in a row.

As it would happen, that's exactly where the rigmarole led. After the kind folks at CNN carefully vetted the top twenty-five hero candidates, they whittled the list to ten, and on the heels of presenting me with the coveted award, it was full-on *Katy bar the door*. A swirling storm of spectacular opportunity was brewing, a storm for which I was totally unprepared.

A few months after the CNN *Heroes* show out in L.A., Daniel and I received a call from ABC—as in, the broadcast company. The person on the other end said she represented the show, *Extreme Makeover: Home Edition*, and that the producers of that show were interested in having us partner with them to do a build. I remember shaking my head silently in disbelief over such a proposition: Carol and I had loved that show for years, and now I was actually going to be affiliated with it?

An army officer, Staff Sergeant Patrick Ziegler, had been injured in a recent shooting at Fort Hood, Texas, and the show wanted to build him a new home as a way of acknowledging all he had endured. As the production assistant filled in the blanks, my mind trailed back to that November 5, 2009, episode. To our country's collective horror, breaking news reported that someone—believed to be a US Army man—had opened fire in the Soldier Readiness Processing Center of Fort Hood in Killeen, Texas, just two hours west of the ranch. Early reports confirmed that people had been fatally wounded and that a whole slew of others were being treated urgently. My initial thought was, *How could members of our country's armed forces be caught unarmed and thus incapable of defending themselves?* only to learn later from Daniel that base regulations across this country supersede state laws allowing concealed carry licenses for enlisted soldiers, airmen, and the like. The folks assembled at Fort Hood that day were fish in a barrel—helpless, easy prey.

For days after that shooting, and as the story settled on me like a shroud, I reflected on the drastic lengths the shooter had gone to in order to prove faithful to his religion. I don't espouse his radicalized beliefs, of course, but the passion he exhibited on behalf of those beliefs was somehow compelling to me. I grew up in an era when most North Americans referred to themselves as "Christian," regardless of the ins and outs of their actual practiced faith. It was normal to believe in God, to talk about God, and astoundingly even to *like* him. These days, the tables have turned. I caught an interview on TV the other day with Larry Gatlin, of The Gatlin Brothers country-music fame, and he summed up where we are as a nation, when it comes to the topic of God. He said that while it seems "reasonable" to offer women the right to choose whether to abort a baby and to alter the definition of marriage and so forth, God has something to say about these issues, and thanks to Scripture, his opinions are quite clear. In the wake of one man going to every length for a belief system he held, deplorable though his actions were, I couldn't help but ponder how well I was defending my own belief system, one that prizes others-centeredness, love in action, the choice for peace and forgiveness even when what seemed warranted were outrage, bitterness, and revenge. The Fort Hood story would test all Christians on these fronts: would we band together and practice forgiveness, or would we raise our fists and load our guns?

In the end, an episode lasting no more than ten minutes would go down in history as the worst shooting ever to take place on an American military base. Thirteen people died and thirty-two others were wounded, all because of one soldier's deplorable actions. It was a tragedy, through and through. Even so, given the calling God had placed on my life, I knew there was a productive way I could respond. I could build one of the survivors a home.

Patrick Ziegler was one of those who had been shot but had survived, and my team immediately rallied to his side. We would soon learn that Patrick had been shot not once but four times—in the head, in the shoulder, in the arm, and in the hip. That first shot he remembered vividly, describing the experience of sitting there in the readiness center upon returning home from his second tour in Iraq and thinking that a drill of some sort had unfolded, when a red beam flashed across his eyes. But on the heels of that beam came a bullet, and that bullet exploded his skull. The traumatic brain injury Patrick suffered was profound and would necessitate doctors removing 20 percent of his brain. In its place, they installed a baseball-size metal plate—hardly a desirable swap.

The team from *Extreme Makeover* planned to construct a new home in Salado, Texas, for Patrick and his wife (who was his fiancée when the shooting occurred) and would reveal the good news to Patrick by hiding in a Bradley tank there at Fort Hood during formation and then popping out to announce the build. As everyone expected, Patrick and his fiancée, Jessica, were surprised and overwhelmed and overjoyed. It was a beautiful moment to behold. The build itself would be completed in one hundred hours, we were told, an ambitious goal we'd never tried to meet before. "Of course we'll do it," Daniel and I said to the producer. "And it will be right. And right on time."

Extreme Fun

Even for a guy who doesn't get starstruck very often, I have to admit it was a real thrill to be on set with Ty Pennington, Paul "Paulie" DiMeo, and the rest of the *Makeover* team. They were kind, gracious, and flexible when it came to the details of the build. They knew my team had been completing homes for injured veterans for some time and as a result were open to our ideas about the designs and features that would most improve Patrick's quality of life. Together, we rounded up vast community involvement, secured a buildable lot, contacted and committed suppliers, and raised necessary funds to complete the four-day build. Concrete was poured at night and then framed the very next day. It was a

ABC *Extreme Makeover* show in Salado, TX

complete madhouse of enthusiasm and activity, but all that hustle paid big dividends. For the waiting audience of well over one million viewers, a good show was produced, a wide beam of spotlight was pointed at wounded veterans, and a mighty fine home was built.

The experience netted positive results for me on a variety of fronts. On a superficial level, it was great fun to see how the television show was put together each time. I knew of the design team's roles and enjoyed watching them at work, but the real delight for me was seeing literally thousands of volunteers work tirelessly day and night from the very center of their expertise. I love watching excellence in action, and this project filled my tank.

A more substantive takeaway had to do with the family who received the home, the Zieglers. Watching the show's producer and design heads interact with the couple taught me the crucial nature of properly vetting potential home recipients in the context of Operation FINALLY HOME. For instance, because of the freshness of Patrick's wounds and issues, he wasn't yet entirely sure what types of accommodations would best enable him to live a productive daily life going forward. If he didn't know his own needs, then he couldn't make those needs known; and if he couldn't make those needs known, then even the best builder in the world simply couldn't design a home to meet them. I walked away from that experience with renewed appreciation for a process that ensures the right deliverable for the right family, at the absolute right time. It would prove a valuable lesson for our organization for years to come.

Ending as We Began

In the same way that 2010 began with a bang, it closed out with equally frenetic activity. Our team was absolutely flooded with media opportunities, once the *Extreme Makeover* show aired. For Daniel and me both, we felt as though we'd been transported to a parallel universe where things like food and sleep were luxuries, not necessities. I had promised him back at the beginning of 2009 that things would start to slow down, but now, almost two years later, I realized I'd flat-out lied to my favorite guy. Nothing about our work was pacing itself; in fact, we were being totally run into the ground. And yet not once did we feel depleted or worn out. If anything, we were just catching our stride.

One of the media opportunities that came our way as a result of working with the *Makeover* team was from the morning news show *Fox and Friends*. Granted, I had several homes under construction, a ranch to run, and what felt like a million other irons in the fire, but how could I say no to the Fox News group? Their viewers are passionate and patriotic and people I deeply wanted to reach. This was an easy yes.

After the Fox News segment ran, word-of-mouth connections were made, eventually prompting a builder in St. Charles, Illinois, to reach out about building a home for a wounded family. Finally! A build outside the state of Texas. I had been hoping for such a turn of events.

Daniel and I flew to Chicago to meet with a local builder and check out the property being considered for the build. While there, my associate received a call from Sharon Gorrell, an influential real-estate agent and lobbyist in the Chicago area who was interested in helping military families—specifically, one in nearby Naperville, Illinois. Two opportunities outside of our home state, occurring at the same time and in the same week? Daniel and I were flabbergasted. Coincidence, to say the least. Or maybe just God's sovereign hand!

Our time in Chicago was a frigid experience, especially for two hot-weather, single-layer men. I didn't own a heavy coat, let alone have one with me, and as a result, I shivered my way through the site visits we made. During our meeting on property with the prospective St. Charles builder, I found myself wading through six inches of snow, and in cowboy boots no less. My feet were frozen and wet, Daniel and I were miserable, and I pretty much wanted to go home. And yet the builder's enthusiasm never once waned. He was determined to build a home for an injured family, snowy day or not.

That evening, Sharon arranged for us to meet with the city council in Naperville. It had been a hectic day, but I was looking forward to an indoor meeting for the simple reason that at last, I could thaw out. The city council meeting began, and I was asked to tell them a little about BABASOT, which I proudly began to do. I described how our program worked, I introduced Daniel as my partner, and I asked if anyone had any questions. Slowly, a frail gray-haired lady rose and said, "Let me get this straight. You guys are from the Bay Area in California, and this man is your partner, as they say?"

Clearly, our "Bay Area" designation needed to change now that we weren't just a Texas shop. And I also clarified that Daniel was my business partner, not my partner in any other sense of the word.

Later that night, as Sharon drove Daniel and me back to the airport, we revisited that lady's comments and had a good laugh. I was slumped over in the passenger seat, nearly asleep after such a long haul. Somehow the conversation shifted to the idea of changing our name—something patriotic, maybe, something easy to feed back. At the time, various military campaigns were being called "operation" this or "operation" that, and perhaps feeding off of that reality, there in the darkness of the interstate, Sharon said, "You should call your work Operation Finally Home."

Sixty seconds prior to her comment, all I could think about was being back home on the ranch in my own bed with my wife. But now my mind was racing. *Yes, yes: Operation Finally Home.* It is so wonderful to have a place to call home, I reasoned. It's a place of comfort and rest. And what could our soldiers possibly need more than a home—for themselves, for their families, for their future?

"That's it," I said to Sharon. "Operation FINALLY HOME."

Leave a Legacy You Love

Spend a few minutes thinking through the following themes, based on the situations and stories from chapter 5:

1. My experience at the builders' conference proved to me that not only failure but also success would stretch a person's faith. How would you describe the ebbs and flows of your own faith journey? What experiences have stretched it most?

2. A clear theme in Scripture is that the Christian life is walked by faith and not by sight. Why do you suppose this is the case? Why is faith required?

3. How comfortable are you walking by faith and leaning into that which you cannot measure, assess, or see? What do you suppose you stand to learn by faith that you could never learn by sight?

6

RUNNING THE RACE
SET BEFORE ME

CERTAIN SEASONS OF my life have left me shaking my head in disbelief over just how fast time flies. The day my older son became a licensed driver comes to mind, given that a split second before, he was toddling around in a diaper with an action figure clutched in each hand. I remember celebrating our tenth wedding anniversary, then our twentieth, and then our thirtieth, wondering how on earth it's possible for decades to roll their way through at such a quick clip. And I look back on the first five years of Operation FINALLY HOME with the same incredulity and awe.

The years 2006 through 2010 happened in fast-forward— surely that has to be the case. Even stacked up against the busiest eras of my custom-homebuilding business, I consider those years unparalleled in their productivity and pace. I was busy. Crazy busy. And yet as I reflect on those times, I can see that not once did I go to bed stressed, agitated, or worn out. There were plenty of nights when I went to bed in a highly emotional state, but those emotions always pointed to more positive things—gratitude for the families I was serving, for instance, and resolution to help many more. At some level, I viewed my investment of time, energy, money, and heart as a tiny repayment for the sacrifices those servicemen and servicewomen had made to protect the freedoms I enjoy. I work in freedom. I worship in freedom. I live in freedom, day by day. For me, each home I was part of building was a real, tangible monument honoring those whose lives had been laid on the line. And so, I pushed. I pushed hard, month after month, year after year, determined to meet more service members, understand their plight, discover their desires, and get them into a home.

The Blessing-Paved Path

Those fast-forward years when Operation FINALLY HOME was getting off the ground gave me fresh appreciation for why one writer referred to the God-centered life as a "race." In Hebrews 12:1-2, the writer says, "Therefore we also, since we are surrounded by so great a cloud of witnesses, let us lay aside every weight, and the sin which so easily ensnares us, and let us run with endurance the race that is set before us, looking unto Jesus, the author and finisher of our faith, who for the joy that was set before Him endured the cross, despising the shame, and has sat down at the right hand of the throne of God."

These verses perfectly depict what I was experiencing real-time, which is that following God's plans really does elicit the same exhilarating euphoria of an all-out sprint, in which you're leaned forward, arms pumping, legs cycling, chest heaving, sweat dripping, elation climaxing as you see that coveted finish line come into view. But perhaps the greater truth in the metaphor is that little phrase tucked into the end of verse one: the race is "set before us," it says, which means this race isn't something we conjure up ourselves. No, the race is something that is placed in front of us and by none other than a loving God. It took me a full five years to feel like I'd sort of caught up to God, despite my having run with all my might each step of the way. But once I did—once I caught up to him and caught my breath, a wide smile taking over my face—I caught sight of what he'd been up to that whole time. The path he'd been laying underneath my sprinting stride was paved not by cement and asphalt but by blessings—one and then another and then another. Perhaps the most profound one of all, as I look back on things today, unfolded for me right at home.

Home Team

I have to imagine it wasn't easy for Carol to set aside our dream of my retirement—which meant slowing our pace, settling down, and finally having a "forever home" of our own—and charging ahead, full-steam, on what felt like the umpteenth wild goose chase of my career. But to her everlasting credit, she barely batted an eye. "God is calling you to this work," she confirmed in her wonderfully declarative style. "And if he is calling you to it, he will provide every last resource to ensure that accomplishes whatever he wills."

Carol's sensitivity to God's movement in my heart and life—as well as her laudable levels of understanding, patience, compassion, and grace—were fuel for my tank during those formative days and years. Her daddy, as I've mentioned, was a Baptist preacher, which meant that Carol was well versed in the ins and outs of "calling." She knew that no human-made scheme or strategy stood a chance of rivaling the fulfillment and soulish satisfaction that shows up when we go God's way instead. Plus, according to her, I had never been quite as passionate about an endeavor as I was with my work with Operation FINALLY HOME. I had to admit that she was right. To my knowledge, nothing has ever captivated my mind, my heart, my schedule, my resources, my best efforts, my best prayers, or my best devotion as has this mission God asked me to accomplish.

From the very beginning, Carol would attend Operation FINALLY HOME events with me, she would encourage me when my to-do list was getting a little long, and she would join me in praying that God would continue to direct our little organization's steps. But equally true, she allowed my calling to remain mine. She was deeply engaged in her own calling—her work with the crisis-pregnancy center in Houston—and she knew that while her voice in my life was the loudest, most beautiful, most inspiring one around, she was careful not to forsake her own spiritual journey, the unique race that God had asked her to run. Her commitment to that race helped me remain committed to mine—on more than a few occasions. It also compelled me to rally to my side additional team members who could help me fulfill our vision, rather than putting inordinate weight on Carol's shoulders to be all things to me.

The Daniel Effect

It is evident that Daniel Vargas and I share a strong connection, tracing all the way back to that very first conversation. Indeed, many of our "wins" link directly back to efforts of his (not the least of which is the CNN *Heroes* show). But I think in the end, the most significant contribution Daniel will have made to Operation FINALLY HOME is the quality people he has magnetized to our cause. For instance, it was Daniel who said we should enlist the aid of Veterans Health Administration (VA) hospital case workers as a means for vetting soldier families who might receive homes, a process we value still today. There are multiple VA hospitals in every state in the Union, as well as in Guam, Puerto Rico, Samoa, the Philippines, and the Virgin Islands. They are ubiquitous, and they are plugged in. If you are a service member injured in the line of duty, you are automatically assigned a VA caseworker. And so when it came time to sort out which service members had the greatest needs and also which were the most motivated to seize future opportunities to overcome their challenges and actually thrive in life, those case workers were a godsend through and through.

Later, when Operation FINALLY HOME grew to a size that it was no longer cute or quirky that its founder, yours truly, didn't possess a checkbook, it was Daniel who said that we should hire an accountant named Ashleigh to manage our books. She was working for a company at the time, and given our cash shortage,

I wasn't too sure it would be anything close to a fair exchange for her to come aboard. Soon enough, to further cloud my vision on the whole deal, she and her husband announced they were pregnant. But Daniel was unrelenting. By this point, Ashleigh had been keeping our numbers straight for some time—serving all but pro bono, I'm embarrassed to say—and knew everything there was to know about our finances. If she got away, we'd have to bring someone up to speed, which would take time, something neither Daniel nor I had right then.

One day, I answered my phone and heard Daniel say, "Hey, brother, I hope you're not mad at me." How's that for a conversation opener?

"Why would I be mad at you?" I asked, to which he said, "Well, I took a big step without running it by you."

Now, he really had my attention. "All right," I said, a little tentatively.

"Ashleigh said she would be willing to work for us if she could work from home so that she wouldn't have to leave the baby every day."

"That sounds reasonable," I told Daniel. "What's the catch?"

"I told her she could be our controller and that she could start tomorrow," he said, making Ashleigh Chesser the second official employee of Operation FINALLY HOME.

All I could do was laugh. The brilliant Daniel Vargas strikes again! Granted, if you phone Ashleigh even during normal business hours, there's a strong chance you'll hear young Annabelle hollering or giggling in the background, but I defy you to find a more conscientious contributor than Ashleigh. She has been a blessing since day one.

Celebrity Endorser, Courtesy of God

It was also Daniel who said I "had to meet" his close friend and partner in crime, J. R. Martinez. The two had been friends for years, after having met at the first event Daniel ever hosted for injured veterans, long before I knew who Daniel was. J.R. had served in Iraq and had been wounded when his vehicle ran over an IED, leaving J.R. trapped inside. He lived, but the impact of the explosion was real. J.R. was left with third-degree burns over 34 percent of his body, centralizing on his face and hands. What's more, the profound smoke inhalation he'd endured had badly damaged his lungs and other internal organs. J.R. thought he would die there in the vehicle, as he was forced to suck down thick clouds of smoke, but God had other plans in mind. And thankfully, they included us.

During J.R.'s recovery, he received outpatient care (and also lived at) Brooke Army Medical Center, in San Antonio, Texas. By then, Daniel had become something of a social planner for Brooke's wounded veterans, and so when one of the case workers there received a call from the production company ABC, asking if they knew of anyone who might be willing to try out for a new role that had been written for the soap opera *All My Children*, Daniel was consulted. The character was a wounded veteran, and the producer decided to try to find the real deal to play the role. Daniel knew just the guy.

Daniel broached J.R. with the idea, who quickly dismissed it and moved on with life. But you know enough of Daniel Vargas by now to know that he wasn't that easily dissuaded. He pestered J.R. day after day until J.R. agreed to fly to New York and try

out. Well, after dazzling the production staff with his easy personality—not to mention intriguing them with "actual" wounds and scars—he was handed the three-month role. Not surprisingly, now that I know J.R. well, that role was expanded, continuing until the day the show left the air.

J. R. Martinez and Dan at Warrior Weekend at ranch in Centerville

From there, J.R. was selected to compete on season 13 of the hit show *Dancing with the Stars,* and again, his personality shone. Ten weeks after that man's dancing debut, he was crowned champion of the whole deal.

Since our inception as an organization, I was adamant about not spending vast sums of money on advertising, promotions, or superstar endorsers, figuring that the last thing I wanted to do was to take in donations for wounded service members, only to turn around and spend that cash not on helping those wounded service members but on paying for TV spots or magazine spreads. There had to be another way. And so, believing what Carol had told me at the start, I waited instead on God to provide the resources we would need and in a way that would fully honor those we were trying to serve. And God did provide. Daniel made the introduction, J.R. and I hit it off, and today, the man is our de facto national spokesperson, even though we've never paid him a dime. He loves our approach to coming alongside men and women who are just like him, and the community of valiant soldiers surely does love him.

Kid Rock? Seriously, God?

With precious little effort on my part, God was assembling a spectacular team around me while simultaneously seeing to the handful of issues that tend to determine whether a young business will mature and thrive or fail: money matters; personnel matters; and people with platforms who were eager to champion our cause. I say "people" because J.R. wasn't alone; in due time, many more performers and celebrities would approach us, asking if there was some way they could get involved. Perhaps the unlikeliest supporter we've attracted along the way is the guy who introduced me at the CNN *Heroes* awards show: Kid Rock—"Bobby" to me.

Robert Ritchie is a brilliant long-haired fortysomething singer, songwriter, rapper, instrumentalist, actor, and marketer who, based on my firsthand knowledge, is prone to toss around some colorful language in the very same paragraph that a thoughtful several-sentence tribute to his life's role model, Jesus Christ, might appear. (In a recent *Rolling Stone* article, which was laced with a little . . . sailor speak, you might say, he did this very thing, commenting on the heels of his vulgarity about how his heroes are: "Jesus. George Washington. And anybody that's had the b**** [we'll call it "courage"] to go and fight for this country."[1] The guy is nothing if not entertaining. And highly unpredictable.)

By way of contrast, I am a sixtysomething nonsinger who has had cropped hair every day of my life. And regarding the tossing about of colorful terms, well, you could just say I don't do that. An improbable pair, we definitely are. And yet I count him one of my dear friends.

Bobby and I met at that CNN show, as you'll recall, and then the following year, CNN called to see if I would attend again. I'd just had rotator-cuff surgery and was hesitant to fly so soon, given the sling I was in that made my elbow stick out like a giant chicken wing, and so I told the producer that regrettably, I was out. The next day, he called back and said, "Mr. Wallrath, I'm calling to ask you to reconsider. Kid Rock will be our evening's entertainment, and he wants you to introduce him. He said he introduced you last year, and now he wants you to introduce him." I was shocked. And also honored. I told him my answer was yes.

The day before the show, I attended a mandatory rehearsal, and as soon as I saw Bobby, I slung a hug around his neck and thanked him for all the added exposure the televised event would provide Operation FINALLY HOME. "Of course, man!" he said with a huge smile. "I believe in what you're about."

Backstage at that event, Bobby and I start scheming about how much fun it would be to collaborate on a project, perhaps in his hometown of Detroit. He passed me his personal telephone number and said, "Let's do it. Give me a call."

More Alike Than I Knew

Several weeks later, I knew it was time to follow up with Kid Rock. I wasn't sure how serious he was about his offer to do a Detroit build together, but I was about to find out. One of the divisional presidents with PulteGroup, one of the nation's biggest homebuilders and also a partner of ours, happened to reside in Michigan, so I quickly looped him in. Daniel had vetted a family—US Army Sergeant Davin Dumar and his wife, Dana, both of whom were from Detroit—and as long as Bobby followed through on his stated intentions, all systems were a go.

In early 2011, Davin was wounded by an IED in Afghanistan and eventually lost his left leg and severely injured his right arm. He underwent *seventy* surgeries and had to relearn how to walk, as a result of the accident, and as his story circulated through media channels, Dana, a passing crush from the couple's high school track team, heard that he was in the explosion and felt compelled to see her old classmate in the hospital. To make a long (and lovely) story short, she hasn't left his side since. The two fell in love and were married in the fall of that year, at Walter Reed Army Hospital, while Davin was still in a wheelchair.

My ever-expanding team gathered all interested local parties

Kid Rock and Dan at his home in Michigan

for a town hall meeting there in Detroit in order to confirm who would be sponsoring and participating in the build, and as things unfolded there, Daniel and I eyed each other with elation. Because of the generosity of everyone present, we were going to accomplish this particular build without incurring a *single* Operation FINALLY HOME expense. What's more, in addition to rallying all sorts of building partners to his side, Bobby said that he himself was going to fund every last finishing touch for the home—the furniture, the window blinds, the sheets and towels, the dishes, the whole bit. And based on what I saw in that finished home a few months later, Kid Rock does not cut corners.

The giveaway of that home was a special event that honored the Dumars and, I truly believe, God. The young couple was awestruck over the attention to detail in their new abode, and my guess is that the smiles they wore that day stayed in place for weeks and weeks following our departure. The experience confirmed practically something I'd known in theory for decades prior—that it really is more blessed to give than to receive. I was floating up with the clouds the entire afternoon, as I pictured Dana and Davin falling asleep that night in a brand-new bed in their brand-new bedroom in their beautiful brand-new home.

Perhaps it was this same sense of soulish satisfaction that

Davin Dumar, Sergeant, US Army, and his wife with
Kid Rock and Dan at home dedication in Michigan

compelled Bobby to turn to Daniel and me toward the end of the giveaway and say, "Hey, why don't you guys come out to my house tonight—have some food, have some conversation, hang out?" As I was telling Bobby that we'd be delighted to come, I noticed that his security guys' faces registered disbelief. "Nobody but family ever comes to his house," they later told me.

We did wind up going to Bobby's house that evening, and my mind was totally blown. For all the bad-boy-persona antics Bobby is known for, his homestead was a place of utter and complete peace. Martha Stewart would have been duly impressed: immaculate furnishings, tasteful décor, and not a single skull-and-crossbones to be found. At some point after our arrival, he took us on a golf-cart tour of his twenty-acre estate, and en route from the main house to his on-property recording studio, we passed a bronze statue of Jesus. Casually, familiarly, Bobby brushed his hand against Jesus' chest as we eased by. "I talk to him every day, Dan," he said. To which I said, "I do too."

Connected and Content

I didn't see it at the time, of course, but in a thousand ways—including connecting me with a Jesus-loving rocker—God was showing me that this calling he'd given me was at its core *his*. It was *his* work I was participating in, *his* vision I was bringing to fruition, *his* mission I was helping accomplish, and *his* assignment I was chasing down. And because all this was his deal (and by definition, then, not mine), he was going to see it through to completion in the way that *he* saw fit.

That line of thinking would help me tremendously over the years to come, primarily because it forced me to keep an open mind regarding who would link arms with us and what our organization's legacy would be in the end. But in those first five years, the most important by-product of remembering whose mission was underway here was this: When you stay tethered to the fact that you are merely God's emissary in this big, bad world, you start to see people not for their superficialities but as prized creations of the most high God. The more I leaned into the fact that I was on a mission by God, the more I wanted not simply to provide shelter for these soldiers but to really know them. I wanted to call them friends.

Back in the fall of 2009, as cooler weather began to unfold in central Texas, Daniel and I had what we believed was a great idea. With the goal in mind of befriending some of our newly sheltered soldiers, we invited twelve of them to the ranch for a weekend getaway. On the premises was an Old West-style bunkhouse that could sleep twenty-five, a hundred-acre lake overflowing with bass, and a plethora of critters and varmints to hunt. We would ask professional fishing guides to donate their time and their boats for the purpose of getting those vets out on the lake, wheelchairs and all, and we would host a huge fish fry every night, assuming the guys actually caught anything.

The more we brainstormed, the more ideas surfaced. We would set up a couple of clay launchers so that guys could practice their shotgun skills, we would invite any willing participants to head out at night with the Rangers and help thin our wild hog population, and we would light up a huge campfire and set out camping chairs and Adirondacks every evening in order to facilitate story-swapping among the men.

With an abundance of enthusiasm and sky-high hopes, we issued that first round of invitations and received all yeses in response. Our first "Warrior Weekend" was a go, and our little team couldn't be more excited.

Beautiful Breakthroughs

Weeks later, our first-ever Warrior Weekend guests arrived—fifteen soldiers, as it turned out, from all across the nation, plus double that many volunteers who'd agreed to come to the ranch on their own dime, just to help serve meals or clean bunk rooms. I'm sure none of us will ever forget seeing an army general scooping out baked beans to those soldiers—and with a broad smile on his face, no less. Pedigreed businessmen, highly ranked military officers, impressive members of various boards of directors—they all came out in droves, eager to do whatever menial task needed doing, all because they wanted to serve the guys who had served us all so well.

I remember meandering through the dining hall or around the campfire during that first weekend, and the stories I'd stumble upon from one guy or another absolutely blew my mind. Most times, they would be talking to each other as I happened by, and just by virtue of being at the right place at the right time, I'd learn about some huge physical challenge one of them was facing, about how one of them was worried about his marriage, or about how they were getting the runaround from the organizations who said they existed to serve our wounded vets. It was obvious to me that the men who had come to our Warrior Weekend were enjoying not just a relaxing getaway and some pretty good chow, but also a deep level of camaraderie they were hard-pressed to find anywhere else. "These guys get me," one of them told me that weekend. "My colleagues, my kids, even my wife—they want to understand what I've been through, but they just can't. But these guys? They've been there too."

We would quickly expand our format to twice annually, and this sense of connectedness, this ready-made environment of empathy and support, was a game changer for every soldier who came to the ranch—not just that weekend, but *any* of the weekends we hosted, spring or fall . . . to date, ten in all. Take the story of a Green Beret, US Army Staff Sergeant John McCrillis. It was at a Warrior Weekend that I would hear his incredible story involving the missions he'd been asked to complete in both Iraq and Afghanistan, one centered on targeting and taking out a key Taliban leader. To this day, John wonders if he somehow received bad intel: as he approached his target, he was ambushed. Two shots to his back and one to his femur left him writhing in pain and fearing for his life.

Within minutes, John was medevaced from the scene by heli-copter, and there at the ranch, he recounted the main memory he holds from that experience. "My wife had given me a James Avery cross necklace before I deployed," John explained, "and as I lay there on the stretcher, I looked down and saw my own blood dripping across that cross. All I could do was think about the price that Jesus paid for my life, for everyone's lives . . . I felt such a sense of gratitude wash over me as I stared at that bloody cross."

John was in agony over his gunshot wounds, but he remembers offering a simple prayer to God that had nothing to do with pain management: "Please, God," he said, "please get me home to my wife and baby. I want to be a good husband and a good father for them."

As soon as the prayer left his lips, John's pain dissolved into a sense of comfort and peace. He knew he was being cared for by a divine agent. He knew he was going to live.

When John returned home, falling into the same predicament as so many wounded warriors, he could not afford housing for his family. He and his wife decided to bunk with his wife's mom, which is how, night after night, a genuine war hero could be found curled up on a too-small living room couch. He fell into a state of depression and struggled to find work, which was his status when we were made aware of his story by the Special Forces Advocacy Group. We couldn't build him a home fast enough. A man of *this* character, risking it all to protect our country's interests . . . I was humbled just talking to him.

From time to time, I'll try to stop the flow of what remains a whirling dervish of activity surrounding me and tell God how I feel about this race he's given me to run. With deep-seated appreciation and total humility before him, I'll simply whisper, "Thanks." All these blessings, all these outright *miracles,* all this fulfillment and satisfaction and joy—the whole deal has left me utterly undone.

Leave a Legacy You Love

Spend a few minutes thinking through the following themes, based on the situations and stories from chapter 6:

1. Have you ever thought of your life as a God-honoring race that can draw out of you the same sense of euphoria of running—even winning—a foot race? How would this type of perspective change your view of the challenges you face day by day?

2. If it's true—and I believe it is—that God sets before us a particular race for us, individually, to run, what would you say is the unique race he has given you?

3. That passage in Hebrews indicates that when we lean into God's presence and power as we run the race he has set before us, we will receive the supernatural ability to "lay aside every weight" and become disentangled from entangling sin and run "with endurance" each step of the way. Which of the three do you need more of today, and why? Are you willing to trust God to provide this for you? Why or why not?

4. Toward the end of the chapter, I commented that the lavish blessings God kept bestowing on me showed me that "the calling he'd given me was, at its core, *his*. It was *his* work I was participating in, *his* vision I was bringing to fruition, *his* mission I was helping accomplish, and *his* assignment I was chasing down. And because all this was his deal (and by definition, then, not mine), he was going to see it through to completion in the way that *he* saw fit." How do you respond to the idea that for the Christ follower, your efforts in life are inextricably linked to a mission that is not yours but God's?

5. What emotions are stirred up as you entertain the prospect of laying down your plans and picking up the will and ways of God? What assumptions, curiosities, concerns, or experiences inform those feelings?

7

TOUGH STUFF

IN 2009, AROUND the same time that my small but ever-expanding Operation FINALLY HOME team and I were planning that first Warrior Weekend in central Texas, twenty-year-old US Air Force Airman First Class Colton Reed, who was stationed at Fort Travis Air Base in California, raised his hand to voluntarily deploy as part of Operation Iraqi Freedom. In every conspicuous way, Colton was the ideal enlisted man. He was young, strong, able bodied—he'd played high school football in Texas, after all—and eager to serve overseas. He filed the required paperwork and waited for the all clear, a go sign that never was to come. The doctor who conducted his physical said that the minor stomach pains Colton had been experiencing necessitated gall-bladder surgery. But the surgery was low-risk and only minimally invasive, the doc explained, and this medical tangent shouldn't at all interfere with Colton's plans for deployment. The date for surgery was confirmed.

On the mid-July morning when Colton was due to report to David Grant Medical Center, he climbed into his car alongside his wife, Jessica, telling her he felt good and that he was relieved the procedure would be straightforward—and quick. Jessica smiled and said she planned to pamper him all day, once the surgery was behind them and Colton had been released.

Half an hour into Colton's surgery, with full confidence that things were going well in the operating room, Jessica headed over to the on-base commissary to get a few groceries. She wanted to make a special dinner for Colton and was giddy as she selected just the right ingredients for her husband. But that dinner would not be made, for upon her return to the hospital, Jessica was informed by the nurse that Colton had been moved to ICU and was in critical condition. Within moments of the surgery's inception, the resident surgeon accidentally nicked Colton's aortic artery, the mainline that supplies blood to extremities from the waist down. The general surgeon blocked the blood supply instead of repairing the artery, and almost immediately, Colton's blood pressure went through the roof. He lost a lot of blood and quickly.

In the waiting room, Jessica tried to remain calm, a feat made all the more difficult once she spotted a nurse down the hall shouting for blood in the OR. Was this her husband's operating room that they were frantic over? Every OR was occupied, but instinctively she knew the answer was yes. While Jessica shot up panicked prayers to heaven, Colton fought for his life. His legs had turned white and then blue, barely registering a pulse each of the three times nurses went for a read. Surgeons worked to keep his blood flowing to his extremities, but it was too late. His legs had died.

Colton Reed, Airman First Class, US Air Force, and Jessica Reed with Governor Rick Perry at his office in Austin

For the next eight hours, Colton lay flatlined, prompting his doctors to transfer him off base. He was taken by emergency helicopter to UC Davis, where a vascular surgeon awaited, and once there, one of the team of doctors who had been assigned to Colton's case told Jessica in grave tones that her husband might not survive. They performed ten surgeries in hopes of saving Colton's legs but ultimately decided to amputate them both, just above his knees. The significant blood loss left him with TBI, a traumatic brain injury, but at least he was still alive.

He remained at Davis for five weeks, receiving sixteen additional surgeries on his legs in which docs removed more and more tissue that had been infected from lack of circulation. In the end, he was left with a three-inch-long right leg and a left leg that ended two inches above where his left knee once had been. The situation was ruled an "extreme" case, which meant Colton was not a candidate for prosthetics. He would be wheelchair bound the rest of his life, all because a routine gall-bladder surgery had taken an unpredictable turn.

Right Jab, Right to the Gut

I would learn of Colton's story from Daniel, who had been put in touch with him by an air force recovery-care coordinator, and the story would haunt me for days. Despite my never having had surgery, gall-bladder or otherwise, never mind a tragically botched surgery like the one he'd endured, I saw myself in Colton's tale. I resonated with a blow from the blind side that life sometimes doles out. Perhaps you've been there yourself: you're cruising along, doing what you do, relishing the bright sun in the sky, and then *bam*, you're surrounded by rain and hail. *Where did* this *storm come from*, you wonder, as you scurry around trying to take shelter. *There wasn't a cloud in the sky!*

For me, the storm erupted the moment I heard my sister Joni's voice on the other end of the phone. "I'm sorry to interrupt your day," she said. "Brother, can you talk?"

She went on to say how much she hated doing this over the phone, but the news just couldn't wait. "It's Mom," she clarified. "That pain in her stomach is a mass."

"Joni," I said, my voice shaky, "what's going on?"

"It's cancer, Dan," she said. "Colon cancer—they're sure." With that, Joni collapsed in waves of tears.

Of my two living sisters—Joni and Pam—Joni has always been the take-charge one. If someone needs help, Joni is the one to drop everything and rush to his or her side. When Mom had fallen ill months prior, Joni took it upon herself to make the hour-long drive to Mom's house every time she needed to get to a doctor appointment. She couldn't bear the thought of Mom doing those visits alone. All us kids adore Mom, but Joni was definitely the most invested in Mom's health. She'd been there for every test, every results report, every specialist consultation, and every ache and pain. And now her patient might not rally . . . it was more than Joni could take.

"They need to do surgery immediately," my sister said quietly, after clearing her throat.

"What do the docs . . . what are they saying?" I couldn't figure out how to appropriately phrase the question that was screaming through my mind: *Is my mom about to die?*

It was just a few stomachaches, I kept thinking. *How can a stomachache turn into this?*

It was just routine gall-bladder surgery, Colton must have said to himself. *How can this come from that?*

I prayed a lot during those long days, when surgery hadn't yet happened and Mom was still in a good deal of pain. "Please comfort her," I'd beg God. "Don't let her be afraid. I know you're already with her, but could you assure her of your presence somehow?"

Carol and I pushed aside our obligations the day before Mom's surgery and drove to the hospital in San Antonio. It's less than a four-hour drive, but it was the longest trip of my life. I couldn't get to Mom's room fast enough. *Please, God, let her live.*

I pushed open the door and found Mom sitting up in bed, a wide smile on her face. "Well, hello!" she said with customary cheerfulness. "Thank you, Danny, for making the trip." Classic Mom. Always warm. Always welcoming. Always putting her kids' needs above her own.

The following morning, as Mom underwent surgery and I walked a marathon pacing those hospital halls, I thought about how strange it was to feel wonderfully blessed on one hand while feeling deeply burdened on the other. My soul was soaring, my family was thriving, and Operation FINALLY HOME was prospering, thanks to those divinely placed opportunities and partners I noted in the last chapter. Life was going so well, and now . . . *this*. Delight and also dread—how on earth was I experiencing both at once?

During those agonizingly long surgery hours, I prayed about as hard as I could ever remember praying for anything in my life. The race God had given me to run felt more like a crawl that day, and how I hate when life is slowed to a crawl—especially a desperate one. Your mind wanders, your hands clam up, your heart races, and you fear the absolute worst. I couldn't help but think back to the time when my wife faced her own cancer scare, back when we were just babies—what, nineteen? Twenty years old? I'd hated the waiting then, and I hated it all the same now. How frustrating it is to be powerless to bring about the end game you desperately want.

Still, in the waiting, God carved out a greater capacity in me to walk by faith, to trust him more. He had proven himself faithful a thousand times before in my life, and I suspected he'd do so again. Even before Mom's doc came out to the waiting room to deliver her surgery results, I noticed a shift in my heart's posture—from anguish and fear to gratitude and joy. "Whatever happens today, Father," I prayed, "I trust you with Mom's life, and with mine."

And Then the Left Hook

"Mr. Wallrath," the surgeon said, as he approached me in the waiting room, "we removed the section of colon where the mass was located, and things went as well as could be expected. The affected area didn't look good, but we'll need to send it out to the lab before I can deliver any definitive results."

Three days later, those lab results were returned, and Mom's tumor was confirmed as benign. Tears sprang to my eyes as a wave of relief washed over me. Mom was going to live. All was well once more . . . or was it?

With my mom's health crisis behind me, I went back to running the ranch and trying to be the best husband, father, granddaddy, and leader for Operation FINALLY HOME that I could possibly be. I was also still trying to make a significant contribution as a volunteer at our church, and the pressures of juggling my professional and personal responsibilities began to take their toll. But I couldn't help but notice that my situation paled by comparison to Daniel's, who was in far worse shape than I was.

I thought back on the time when, about a year into the relationship that Daniel and I had begun with LP Building Products, one of the world's largest manufacturers of building supplies, LP was so pleased with our work with their corporate headquarters based in Nashville that they decided to take our involvement national. The VIPs over at LP drafted up all sorts of agreements for us to sign, saying that they were "elated" and "proud" to be officially partnering—across their entire organization—with Operation FINALLY HOME. It was only after all the signatures were in place that they discovered our staff consisted of two guys and a stay-at-home mom. One of the executives couldn't hide his disbelief: "All the work you've done with us and for us . . . it's just *you* two behind all of that?" I'd never stopped to consider that for a good chunk of Operation FINALLY HOME's history, Daniel and I were doing the work of about fifteen able-minded folks. We were having such a ball that we'd never bothered with keeping track of all the blood, sweat, tears, and hours we were investing in those families we loved. Had we been foolish all that time, taking ourselves for some kind of tireless superhuman breed? Based on what I was witnessing with my colleague, I feared the answer was yes.

Daniel was working through some ongoing struggles as a result of his divorce and was worried about how the transition was affecting his beloved daughter, Raini. What's more, he has a form of multiple sclerosis that was brought on by his service in Desert

Storm and Desert Shield. His hands and feet are turning inward, which is a painful and, according to his docs, unavoidable process. Lots of conditions can cause MS flares, such as fatigue, infection, and hot weather, but based on what all the experts say, topping the list is *stress*. And despite our deep passion for our work, not to mention the gratifying results of our efforts unfolding all around us, one thing we've always had plenty of is good, old-fashioned stress. Which for Daniel meant several surgeries, the loss of his ability to walk and to write, and a stern warning from his doctor that if he didn't give his adrenal system a break—and soon—he would land himself in a wheelchair for the rest of his days. More times than I can count, I would call Daniel to check in on a family or a build and, noticing ambient noise, ask, "Where are you, my friend?" to which he would mumble, "At the VA." I'd ask if everything was okay, but all I'd get in response was an inarticulate, "Mwummwum." All those celebrated blessings from God—were they adding up to a curse for Daniel somehow?

Almost from day one, Daniel had been my sounding board, my confidant, my right hand, and the strongest advocate military families ever could hope to have. What would Operation FINALLY HOME do if Daniel weren't in the mix? As soon as the question entered my mind, I banished it. The truth was, I couldn't bear such a thought.

This Is Provision?

The Bible is full of reminders that one of God's favorite pastimes is providing lavishly for those whom he loves. Truly, you'd have to *want* to miss this theme, to read his word and not see it there. "And my God shall supply all your need according to his riches in glory by Christ Jesus," the apostle Paul says, in Philippians 4:19. Prior to that, he would write that God is able to make "all grace" abound for us, that we might have "an abundance for every good work" (2 Corinthians 9:8). "Therefore I say to you, do not worry about your life," Jesus says, "what you will eat or what you will drink; nor about your body, what you will put on. Is not life more than food and the body more than clothing? Look at the birds of the air, for they neither sow nor reap nor gather into barns; yet your heavenly Father feeds them. Are you not of more value than they? Which of you by worrying can add one cubit to his stature?" (Matthew 6:25-27). And in Matthew 7:7-8, Jesus also says, "Ask, and it will be given to you; seek, and you will find; knock, and it will be opened to you. For everyone who asks receives, and he who seeks finds, and to him who knocks it will be opened."

The prophet Jeremiah said that God has thoughts of "peace and not of evil" toward us, to give us "a future and a hope" (Jeremiah 29:11). And then there is this sentiment, from the prophet Malachi, speaking on behalf of God: "Try Me now in this, if I will not open for you the windows of heaven and pour out for you such blessing that there will not be room enough to receive it" (Malachi 3:10). "Give, and it will be given to you," Jesus says, "good measure, pressed down, shaken together, and running over will be put into your bosom. For with the same measure that you use, it will be measured back to you" (Luke 6:38).

On and on it goes, the litany of proof that God promises he will provide for us, that he indeed does provide for us, and that truly, nothing gives him greater pleasure than to meet the needs of his kids. And yet, when it feels like the bottom is falling out of our lives, even the most faithful among us wonder if these very true things really are true. Or that's how I felt, anyway, during one particular season of Operation FINALLY HOME's young existence, when challenges were mounting, not just on the personnel side, but financially as well.

It started when US Army National Guard combat engineer David Maiolo arrived at his home in New York with his wife and five kids one Sunday morning to find a foreclosure notice on his front door. David had helped with security efforts at Ground Zero following 9/11 and had spent a year as an infantryman in Iraq, which is where he suffered a lower-back injury and became

disabled. To add insult to injury, he began wrestling with symptoms of PTSD. There in New York, he was desperately trying to
get his life back together. And now this.

David and his family lived in an old Victorian home that he
had bought from a woman who had a note at the bank. The agreement made was that the Maiolos would make payments to the
owner, and that she would in turn forward the monies to the bank.
The Maiolos quickly settled into their new abode, even remodel-
ing the entire home prior to David's deployment. They happily
made their mortgage payments, never missing a single one, even
as those checks never quite got to the bank. "We will be auction-
ing off your home as a foreclosure," the bank manager informed
David, when he called to register his disbelief.

The Maiolos reached out to their congressman, the VA, and
both local and state housing authorities, but their efforts were in
vain. They had no legal recourse against the bank and thus had no
one to turn to for help. That is, until David's sister-in-law phoned
him and said, "Why don't you just call that cowboy from Texas?
You know, the one we saw on the CNN *Heroes* show?"

The next day, David's wife sent an e-mail to Daniel, crossing
her fingers that it would go through, and shortly thereafter, Daniel
dialed my number, armed with information I'd find shocking and

David Maiolo, Sergeant, US Army, and family in New York

inspiring alike. "The bank guys are treating a wounded war vet this way!" Daniel's voice boomed in my ear. "We have to jump in and help."

Daniel was well aware that David's situation was beyond the scope of our typical assist. We'd done plenty of builds by then, but simply funding a home purchase? This was uncharted territory for sure.

"Forty-three grand," Daniel said to me, after I asked him what the rescue would cost. He further elaborated that we had exactly forty-five thousand in the bank; this save would take nearly every penny we had to our name. Daniel placed a call to the lawyer who managed the bank's legal affairs to request a little leniency, but, in his words, his client "wouldn't budge."

Two builds that were underway at the time complicated our decision regarding whether to float the forty-three grand. Those houses needed funding, and if we helped out the Maiolos, we'd have nothing to throw their way.

"It just doesn't add up," I remember telling Daniel, even as I knew we were totally in. We couldn't knowingly let a war hero go homeless. We had to step in and help.

The morning we called David on speakerphone to divulge the secret we'd successfully kept—"You can rip up your mortgage note, because that home you're in is *yours!*"—David fell silent, and his wife literally threw up.

Anybody with a lick of business sense would have looked at that and scores of other financial decisions we made across the years and shake their head in disbelief, and perhaps a little pity. *Poor idiots. They don't have a clue what they're doing!* And in terms of the sheer numbers—the assets and the liabilities, the income versus the expenses, and the numbers-never-lie bottom line—they'd be dead right. But what black-and-white balance sheets don't show is that little X factor called *faith*. We always had a sneaking suspicion that regardless of how bleak things looked in our bankbook, God was going to find a way through. To date, despite more than a few renegade moves—not the least of which was draining our account for Mr. Maiolo, whom we'd never officially met—we have never not paid a bill that was due; we have never been late on a payment that was due; and we have never gone into debt. Each time our circumstances have left me curious about whether God would pull through, the answer has come back *yes*. *This,* God would say, time and again, *This is provision.*

You may recall that the two years prior, we had received generous donations at the North American Petroleum and Engineering conference held in Houston—$25,000 the first year and $50,000 the next. We were coming up on the annual event just as we let go of the forty-three thousand and wondered if maybe, just maybe, NAPE would see fit to help us out again.

Convention organizers contacted Daniel weeks prior to the conference to ask for help. They needed an entertainer for the event and were still coming up short. Along the way, Daniel had met Steve Emily, LeAnn Rimes' manager, and so he placed a call, asked a favor, and within hours was able to confirm for NAPE LeAnn's participation. Following LeAnn's spectacular performance on the closing night of the event, Daniel and I were called onto the stage so we could give away yet another home to a very surprised injured vet and his family. The crowd of fifteen hundred went bananas, applauding the soldier's efforts and cheering for his wife. LeAnn was crying. I was smiling so hard I thought I might break my face, and the NAPE organizers were just shaking their heads in gratitude for this amazing thing they were witnessing.

As we made our way off the stage and back into the crowd, the emcee stopped us, saying, "Hang tight, gentlemen. Not so fast." He asked us to join him center-stage, and then he proceeded to make the kind of announcement to the crowd that would cause even an atheist to bend a knee in deference to what was so clearly an intervention from God. "This year," he said to those gathered, "We at North American Petroleum and Engineering have decided that instead of parsing our charitable contribution across several organizations, we would donate the entire sum to just *one* organization." Daniel and I eyed each other, having no idea where this thing was headed.

"And so," the emcee continued, "it is with great delight that we announce this year's *singular* recipient of the NAPE award, totaling *$225,000* . . . Operation FINALLY HOME!"

At that announcement, my heart actually stopped. Or it sure felt like it, anyway. As the crowd went berserk a second time, Daniel and I hugged and laughed and said simply, "Thank you, God."

The Silver Lining We All Seek

A few days after Colton Reed was discharged from UC Davis, where he had endured five long weeks of rehab following his botched gall-bladder surgery, he and his wife left California and headed for Texas, where Colton would undergo further rehabilitation at Brooke Army Medical Center in San Antonio. He was exhausted, stressed, disillusioned, and still in great pain. What's more, he was flat broke. Under the Feres doctrine, which protects service doctors, the Reed family could not sue for medical malpractice because Colton's surgery had taken place on a military base. Colton was seen as a low-level enlisted man, and although he did have standard-issue insurance, he was denied the coverage

LeAnn Rimes presenting check at Nape Expo
in Houston, TX

he needed. Traumatic Servicemembers' Group Life Insurance is reserved for those who injuries were sustained during combat or conflict; Colton didn't fit the bill.

Once at BAMC, Colton's caseworker worked to help him assimilate to life in a rehab hospital, and Colton's wife, Jessica, did everything in her power to meet her husband's needs and soothe his mounting anger and depression. They turned to several organizations that come alongside wounded veterans in times of need, but time and again, doors were shut in their face. It seemed nobody wanted to help a wounded vet who had been wounded in such an obscure way. He wasn't a war hero. He wasn't a Purple Heart recipient. He'd had no daring escape from an IED explosion. He'd just had *gall-bladder* surgery, for heaven's sake. What kind of story was that?

Well, evidently, God thought Colton's story was every bit as exciting as anyone's, and so he started making divine connections, one person to another to another, until at last we caught wind of Colton's situation and all too eagerly jumped into the fray. We decided to build the Reeds a home—right then and there, right away.

Daniel set about contacting Dan Koschner, a high-level executive with land developer Bluegreen Communities, who would later be acquired by Southstar Communities of Austin, Texas. Not surprisingly, they had land available in nearby New Braunfels, and after hearing of the Reeds' dilemma, they said that not only would they donate the lot we needed but knew of the perfect builder for the job. Daniel and Dan Koschner met with that builder, Jimmy Jacobs, and shortly thereafter, Jimmy called and said, "If Bluegreen is donating the lot, then I will donate the build." And just like that, we were underway.

Before building commenced, Daniel met with Jimmy to pass along some of the things we learned over the previous years while building homes for wheelchair-bound individuals. I wanted this home to have the standard fare—lowered countertops, sinks, light switches, and doorknobs, as well as wide hallways and entrances to each room—but there was more I hoped to do. Colton had an automatic lift in his vehicle that would extract his wheelchair for him, but when the lift is operating, the overall situation is too big to fit in a standard-size garage. The net effect was that even in the pouring rain Colton would be out in his driveway waiting on his wheelchair, while getting soaking wet. He needed an oversized garage. Furthermore, I wanted it to be beautiful. This needed to be not merely a utilitarian environment for a person in a wheelchair but a custom masterpiece that would bring peace to Colton's soul each time he entered the space. As Daniel passionately conveyed my vision, Jimmy simply nodded and smiled. He was tracking with me far more than he let on, the proof of which emerged within a matter of months. Jimmy and his crew spared no expense in building a real gem of a home. Gorgeous limestone, thick wood beams, granite countertops, state-of-the-art cooking appliances—the house was breathtaking all the way through. During my walk-through, I took note of one handcrafted pocket door after another, a simple and elegant touch that kept Colton from having to navigate knobs and hinges. Outside, a wide wrap-around sidewalk surrounded the property, a perfect setting from which Colton and Jessica could enjoy views of the scenic hill country.

The couple had wanted children for quite some time, but given Colton's prolonged blood and oxygen loss, he was left unable to father a child. Yet another dream dashed. And yet Jessica was undeterred. She and Colton decided that in vitro fertilization was the next logical step, even as they had no money to pay for such a procedure. They had no cash themselves, and their military insurance didn't cover the treatment in full. Several weeks after the Reeds moved into their new home, Daniel sat with them in their living room, marveling at how well Colton had adjusted to his new environment, and gave them the good news. Daniel and I had talked it over and decided that we needed to step in, make a few calls, and raise the necessary funds for their IVF treatment. The look on Jessica's face said, *If you had told me a year ago that some lanky cowboy from Texas was going to put my husband and me in a brand-new home and then see to it that the fertility treatment I would need (because Colton would have become a bilateral amputee and thus incapable of fathering a child) would be covered, I would have laughed you out of the room. And yet look what has happened. Thank you, God. This*—this *is provision.*

I stay in touch with Colton still today and always come away from our conversations immensely grateful for our enlisted men and women. People like Colton remind me that even when the going gets tough—even when it feels like life can't get any harder, the days can't get any longer, and nobody sees you and nobody cares—there is a silver lining on every single dark, stormy cloud. We really can rise again, even after our circumstances knock us down. We really can prevail on the heels of facing ridiculous tragedy and pain.

This is information I would cling to a few years later, when I suffered a blow I feared would end it all for me. The challenges I'd known would seem like a cakewalk by comparison, as all hell decided to break loose.

Leave a Legacy You Love

Spend a few minutes thinking through the following themes, based on the situations and stories from chapter 7:

1. One of the reasons I resonate with Colton Reed's story is that on many occasions I too had been cruising along in life, believing things were all on the up-and-up, when out of nowhere a storm overtook my skies and I was caught unprotected and unprepared. Can you relate to that feeling?

If so, what were the circumstances for you? How did you handle the situation? Like me, did you happen to turn to prayer?

2. What is your reaction to my assessment of one of the most severe storms I faced, when my mom was diagnosed with cancer: "In the waiting, God carved out a greater capacity in me to walk by faith, to trust him more"? When have you seen this dynamic unfold in your own life: something difficult actually benefiting you in the end?

3. What thoughts or feelings did you experience upon reading of God's commitment to provide for our needs, such as in Philippians 4:19, "And my God shall supply all your need according to his riches in glory by Christ Jesus," and Malachi 3:10, which says, "Try Me now in this, if I will not open for you the windows of heaven and pour out for you such blessing that there will not be room enough to receive it"? What fears or concerns do you have about trusting God more fully to provide for the needs you face?

8

THE KNOCKOUT PUNCH

WITH EACH INJURED serviceman, each servicewoman, and each military family, there has come a uniquely beautiful yet tragic story. The vast majority of the people I've come across, however, have been reticent to share the "tragedy" portion of their journey, but of course it is there. As a builder of mortgage-free homes for wounded veterans, I wouldn't be crossing their paths if it weren't. I see the tragedy in disillusioned countenances. I see the tragedy in stressed relationships. I see the tragedy in strained finances. I see the tragedy in bloodied knuckles of those confined to wheelchairs, still learning how to steer clear of the walls. And with each observation of tragedy, I see a flash of wistfulness in that soldier's eye, the look that says, *I wish this weren't my reality . . . but it is.*

Both parts of that sentiment are critical: the acknowledgment of the awfulness of it all and also the decision to accept things as they are. It's a posture that says, *I hate this pain, but I'm coming to terms with it.* It's a posture that, due to a wild set of circumstances on my horizon, I would soon need to adopt myself.

Good Times

Our decision to relocate to Champion Ranch and take over ranch operations for my dad was, at the time, a pretty straightforward move. We'd thought about it. We'd prayed about it. And we were committed to making it work. In all candor, my homebuilding business was starting to wane, and with the prospect of patching up my relationship with my dad at hand, mine was an easy yes. Plus, I liked the feeling of being responsible for keeping the ranch in the family; it felt good for Dad to trust me like that. The old man was in his eighties now, and it seemed like he'd really made a positive change in his life. The way I saw it, God was slowly closing doors in Houston and slowly opening doors in Centerville. My job was just to walk on through.

The first few years at the ranch were fine. Better than fine, actually. Dad had turned over all aspects of ranch management to my care and was working on a formal plan through which he would legally transition everything to me and my siblings. He repeatedly told me he wanted to keep the ranch in the family, and he recognized that if he held onto the ranch right up until his own demise, we'd get stuck with a giant tax bill and have to sell the ranch in order to pay the taxes. So he decided to transfer the holdings while he was here to see it all happen—and in a manner that protected as much of his net worth as possible.

My father's attorney, Robert, was also his close friend. There was a lot of back-and-forth as various versions of "the plan" were drawn up, and I remember being impressed by how patient and thorough Robert was during the entire process. Whenever Dad's past fiery personality would make an appearance, Robert would quietly explain things as he saw them. "But if you're not pleased with that, Dick," he'd say in highly self-controlled tones, "I can take another run at it." Dad, Robert, and Dad's accountant eventually finalized "the plan," and Robert drew up all the paperwork for Dad and us to sign.

Things seemed to be humming right along—that is, until they came to a screeching halt.

From Good to Bad and Then to Worse

During those first years, I was constantly on the lookout for opportunities to talk to my dad about God. I knew Dad had made useful shifts in his habits and priorities—not the least of which was staying sober—but personal experience had taught me that there was only so much progress to be made by way of human effort. The real gains came only through Jesus Christ. And so I'd pray for Dad each morning, asking God to provide an "open door" that day, as the apostle Paul says to do in Colossians 4:3, for us to talk about spiritual things.

My brother, Mike, shared my desire to see Dad come to faith in Jesus, and we decided that in addition to praying for our father, we would see if he was open to praying with us. For a time, miraculously, he was. Dad, Mike, and I would convene every morning in the ranch office, fill mugs with hot coffee, and sit down to pray for the day's meetings, for any needs in our lives, and so forth. Those prayer times weren't long-lived, but they will always hold a special place in my heart. Nothing makes a man seem stronger than when he is actively dependent on almighty God.

One morning, Mike and I gathered for our prayer meeting with Dad as usual, but Dad never showed. The next morning, my brother and I went to the office at the appointed time, but still: no Dad. I asked my father about his absences when I ran into him on the ranch, but he waved me off, saying something about being too busy. As days turned into weeks and weeks morphed into months, I noticed an increased agitation in him. He'd reprised his old ways of storming around, hollering demands, and cussing out anyone in his path, and I feared the positive changes he'd made were being erased, one by one. Were we headed back to the tyranny I'd known as a terrified kid? That reign hadn't ended well.

The beginning of the end came about one afternoon when I

was in the office tending to paperwork. My dad wanted to review some invoices that we'd already paid and seemed dissatisfied with anything the rest of us did or said. It got heated between my dad and Mike, culminating with my dad blowing out of the office, the door slamming shut in his wake. I sat in my desk chair stunned. What was happening to all the ground we'd gained?

The weeks following the incident with Dad in the ranch office were awkward, but I had no idea just how strained our relationship had become until the day I received a piece of certified mail that removed all hope for reconciliation. It was a letter from my father's new attorney, informing me that I was being sued. My siblings received their notices on the same day.

In our minds, the whole idea—moving to the ranch, reorganizing ranch operations to be running the day-to-day, Dad selling the ranch to us kids while he was still living, and drawing up the contracts the way he did—all of it had been Dad's idea, and yet now we were being sued. I reflexively shook my head as I read paragraph after paragraph of that lawyer's correspondence. By now I had become all too familiar with the casualties of war in our world—the soldiers who come back in pieces and are never the same again. And while I've never stared down a suicide bomber or raided a terrorist's bunker, I can tell you that the war my dad waged against us that day would rip out a part of me I'd never get back.

It wasn't just that I wanted our personal and professional situation at the ranch to work; I *needed* it to work. I'd been searching my whole life for my father's approval, and there—in a leadership seat of the ranch he himself built, in close proximity to the "new and improved" man, and in his good graces at last—I believed I'd found it. I'd walked away from attempting to rebuild my own business, the work I'd poured three decades of time, energy, innovation, and passion into, in order to link arms with my dad because I just knew it was the means to our great end. Somewhere deep inside of me still lived that little boy, age six, being yanked out of first grade midmorning and led alongside his eight-year-old brother to the back of Dad's pickup truck, loaded up in the dead of winter with nothing more than a threadbare blanket to fend off the icy Indiana air, driven the thirty miles into Indianapolis (where Dad's job site was), handed a heavy hammer and a hardware-store nail apron that wrapped around my small waist twice, and told, "Come behind the carpenters and finish the nails."

"Gonna make you boys men if it's the last thing I do," Dad would say to us with slurred speech, nearly every time we made that trip. And I for one believed him. My dad was working as a carpenter, and so I would work as a carpenter too. I would be the best six-year-old carpenter there ever was, if it meant I'd be seen—and valued—by him. But I hadn't felt seen or valued then, and I didn't feel seen or valued now. For the months leading up to the court date, despite the fact that our houses were not even four miles apart as the crow flies, we didn't exchange a single word. My dad was interviewed one time by a reporter who asked him about how he overcame alcoholism and, in a reflective moment, said, "When you're hung up on alcohol, you're living in hell." I'd been through years and years of that particular hell with my dad, back when I was a boy, and now, during those pretrial months when nary a word was spoken between father and son, it felt like we'd headed right back to that fiery furnace where everything goes to die.

The Court Date Nobody Wanted to Keep

The year 2015 found my siblings and me hip-deep in the trial brought against us by our very own flesh and blood, and none of us was handling it very well. In keeping with the roles we've all played since we were kids trying to cope with an abusive alcoholic father, Mike slid into sarcasm. I tumbled toward anger. Joni pecked at us like a mother hen corralling her chicks, and Pam grew literally sick and tired. Pam had been diagnosed with Lupus years prior, brought on by stress incurred when the youngest Wallrath child, our baby sister, Dee Dee, died. Dee Dee was the unanimous favorite in our home, and when she passed away, she took with her whatever small slice of stability we enjoyed. Now, whenever life became too intense, Pam's disease intensified as well, perhaps a divine barometer intended to signal the rest of us to calm things down. "I can't keep doing this," Pam would tell me through tears, during our near-daily phone calls between my office at the ranch and her family's Fort Worth home. I so badly wanted to put the whole ordeal behind us, but I didn't want to play the part of the fool. Dad had enveloped all us kids—not to mention our spouses and our own children—into ranch life to the point that to lose the trial would mean outright financial destitution for every last one of us.

Dad took the stand during the trial, explaining that he had been on new meds when he decided to turn over the ranch assets to his children in a discounted transaction, and that he was confused and "not himself" when the paperwork was signed. In the end, after the lot of us were dragged for three weeks through family-dysfunction muck and mire so gross that it made Pam's health plummet even further, a settlement was reached. Some things just aren't worth the fight. And so it was, that on an otherwise beautiful day in May 2015, all of us Wallraths, save for Dad and his second wife, Patsy, packed up our belongings and under police supervision departed from the ranch.

"I still love each one," Dad had said on the witness stand, in response to his lawyer's question about how he felt about his children and grandson owning the ranch. "But they and the lawyer and the accountant betrayed me and took from me what I had worked for all my life. I ruined my children with money. I harmed them because I let them miss the growth that can come from being responsible."

To be called a betrayer by the man I once admired most in the world and thus set my sights on emulating was a real kick in the gut for me. Regardless of everything we've been through, I would never knowingly betray my dad. Far from it! The loyalty I felt toward him was unwavering, if not totally misplaced. Based on the success of those early months after Carol and I had relocated to the ranch, my heart had zoomed ahead to a future of camaraderie and peace. Toward that deeply desired end, I installed monthly family dinners, where all of us would gather together at the saloon with covered dishes in hand and over barbecued meats, beans, salads, and desserts would enjoy unrushed conversation together. It was a real contrast from the dinner hour of my youth, when Dad was nowhere to be found, and so each time we all showed up for that meal, I silently gave thanks to God for redeeming those years of pain.

From time to time, I'd eavesdrop on my dad as he told one person or another about how proud he was of my leadership there at the ranch. He'd boast in my oversight, saying that what he had worked so hard for all his life had finally paid off, now that he had his whole family together on the ranch. I'd sneak peeks of his broad smile with his shoulders tossed back in pride; his posture that seemed to say, *Look at how we Wallraths made it through! Every family should be as fortunate as ours!* and I'd nearly faint from the ecstasy I felt. *Dad is proud of me!* My shocked inner voice would shout. *It's true! It's really true!* I grew up on the TV series *Father Knows Best* and figured that based on how well things were going those days, the Andersons would have nothing on us. Had Jim and Margaret, Princess, Bud, and Kitten still been around, *they* would have taken cues from *us*.

The slower, quieter environs of the ranch afforded me uninterrupted time to sit with my thoughts, and once a positive trajectory had been set with my dad—*It's a new day! He's a new man! We can begin again as father and son!*—I began to daydream about family vacations with Dad and Patsy, something I'd never heard of as a kid, let alone been on. I pictured all of us—my dad and step-mom, my siblings, my wife, and all of Dad's grandkids—aboard a giant cruise ship pointed toward sun and wind and smiles. Pointed toward the happy ending I believed we deserved.

But then I got the paperwork announcing the lawsuit. And the jolt back to a hapless reality. And the realization upon waking each day that it had all only been a dream.

Where God Is When It Hurts

There's a fascinating story in the Bible about the prophet Elijah, who lived in the kingdom of northern Israel in the ninth century BC. This was during the reign of King Ahab, a man who worshiped false gods, dismissing entirely the God of Israel, Yahweh. King Ahab went so far as to build a temple for Baal, the false god, which incited the faithful Elijah. Under the Lord's direction, Elijah went to Ahab and told the king that because of the evil he had done in the sight of the Lord, there would be years and years of drought so severe that not even dew would fall during that time (see 1 Kings 1:1). The meaning of this threat was surely not lost on Ahab, given that Baal was not only the Canaanite god of rain, thunder, and lightning, but also of *dew*. But still, Ahab blew off the prophet, blew off the warning from God, and continued on his merry way.

This was an errant move, for sure.

The Lord did as his prophet had promised, the drought did come, and for three years, Ahab and his entire kingdom suffered mightily as a result. But the part of the story that gets me the most is this one little side note that you'd almost miss if you read the account too quickly. Right in the middle of God giving Elijah instruction about the terrible drought to come and about what he is supposed to say to the king of the land, he slips in this detail: "Get away from here and turn eastward . . . I have commanded the ravens to feed you there" (1 Kings 17:2-4).

It's almost as if God is saying, *Look, it's all about to come tumbling down around you, but I've carved out a protected place for you, Elijah. My provision still will be yours.*

When life came tumbling down for me in 2015, I thought about that prophet and about the lunacy of believing that a *bird* would keep him from death. And yet wouldn't you know it: the ravens came, they delivered bread to the starving man, and he thrived in a day when crops and people and hope itself were all fighting (and failing) to stay alive.

I've been asked on several occasions since the grenade of that lawsuit was dropped in my lap to explain why God would allow all the abuse, all the drama, all the chaos the way he did, only to culminate with ostracism and pain. And to those questions, my response has been the same: "God only knows."

My answer is evidence of cynicism and also of comfort. *God only knows why I'd be asked to walk through so much pain!* And also, *God only knows why I'd be asked to walk through so much pain.* The latter of those two is more important here; I can't explain the journey I've been on, but God can. What solace I take in that fact. God knows where I have been, where I am, and where I am going. He knows his plans for me, and regardless of what my earthly father says, they don't involve destitution and pain. My heavenly Father's plans for me center on giving me "a future and a hope," Jeremiah 29:11 promises, and my plan is to take him at his word.

The wound from this last battle with my dad is still fresh, and so perhaps it's a little premature for me to try to make sense of the shrapnel just yet. But I will say this: across the twelve months that have elapsed since leaving the ranch for what I presume was my final departure, I have known a closeness, an intimacy, with God that I have never before known. I have sought his wisdom with greater fervency, lingered in prayer with greater patience, extended grace to others with greater intention, and seen his provision for the lifeline it is. What's more, I have embraced the valiant soldiers I've met with a different level of compassion because, now more than ever, I can relate to what it feels like to be at war. In a thousand ways, those strong, survival-oriented women and men have been my ravens, passing me vital crumbs of sustenance when I was sure I would starve and die.

And maybe that's the lesson here I keep trying to learn; as long as I'm alive, I ought to choose to keep on living. While life is still choosing me, I pray I'll be wise enough to keep choosing life.

Leave a Legacy You Love

Spend a few minutes thinking through the following themes, based on the situations and stories from chapter 8:

1. Despite all of the blessings I've known, of course there remains tragedy just beneath the surface of my life, remembrances of times when the sun wasn't shining, hope seemed hidden, and my usual smile was nowhere to be found. As you reflect on your own life, what struggles, challenges, or other unwanted baggage have you picked up along the way that you wish just weren't part of your present reality?

2. How have you "made peace" with those things that have weighed you down? Or does peace elude you still today?

3. How does my explanation of my own pain that "God only knows" sit with you? Is this idea comforting or troubling: no challenge we face catches God off guard?

4. Do you suppose there are "ravens" nearby ready to feed you in the same way I received sustenance in my time of deepest need? What might it sound like for you to call out to God, asking him to make good on his promise to give you everything you need for health and life? Consider writing out your prayer.

ALIVE DAY

JUST PRIOR TO all of those shenanigans with my father—this would have been mid-2012—thirty-year-old California native US Army Staff Sergeant Monte Bernardo led his 82nd Airborne Division team into an area south of Kandahar, Afghanistan, whereupon they would be ambushed and forced up a berm.

This was not Monte's first wartime excursion; he'd been to Iraq already, as well as to a different part of Afghanistan, serving as a cavalry scout who led his squad on patrols, navigation outings, and widespread searches for bombs. So far, so good, in terms of making it out of those experiences alive and with all key pieces intact. But this time, on this particular tour, his luck, unfortunately, would run out.

Back on the embankment, Monte's team waited, watching with heightened awareness for any activity, as Monte braced himself with his left hand and slid to a seated position. He heard a loud noise followed by a distinct quaking sensation, but before he could sort out what was going on, the bomb beneath him had gone off. On Independence Day that year, Monte lost nearly every bodily freedom he'd known. His hand was blown off. His two legs were blown off. And the jokester's ever-present smile, for the moment, was gone.

Life Left to Live

Four days later, Monte woke up in an ICU hospital bed at Water Reed Medical Center in Bethesda, Maryland, where he would soon endure multiple surgeries and a whole lot of physical therapy sessions. Within forty-seven days, the PTs and OTs would have him walking steadily on prosthetics, but regaining some sense of normalcy would be a more challenging goal to attain. As Monte's girlfriend, his eleven-year-old daughter, and his siblings cheered the strides Monte was making—he could walk! he could cook! he could handle everyday life!—Monte himself was vastly more subdued. With these injuries and this hamstrung existence, how would he get a job and afford to live?

My team and I learned of Monte's situation and knew immediately that we wanted to help, and as we got to know Monte firsthand, that desire only grew. Here was a guy who was so unusually upbeat about his tragic circumstances that, in response to the persistent questions of friends, family, military personnel, and reporters, he could be heard saying things like, "I'm just glad it was me and not one of my squadron mates." And, "If selfless service to this country meant going through what I'm going through, I'd do it all over again." And, referring to the day of the explosion that took his good hand and both legs, "Yeah, it was a bad day, but at least I still have this!" He'd then hold up his left arm, wave his left hand, and grin.

A "bad day"? Who thinks like that?

Monte Bernardo—that's who.

When Monte goes to bed every night, it is with the ringing of sirens and automatic-weapon fire in his ears. When he wakes up every morning, he stares down at stumps for legs. When he leaves his house to go get groceries or the mail, he has to factor in extra time, to accommodate the stiff prosthetics that don't allow smooth ambulation like real legs do. In a thousand day-to-day scenarios, he absorbs the gawking and presumptive questioning from onlookers who have no idea what he has been through. And yet every time I've encountered the man, he has been bubbled over with gratitude for the fact that he's still taking in oxygen, mentally sharp, and has life left to live. "That day didn't beat me!" Monte says. "It tried, but it didn't win."

Soldiers who have been wounded in battle refer to the day they defied death as their "Alive Day," the day when they came way too close to death but made it out alive. They may have been robbed of some of their body parts. They may have had a slice of their mental functioning

Fioreamante "Monte" Bernardo, Sergeant, US Army, getting ready for one of his many outings

taken from them. They may have watched buddies get blown to smithereens mere feet from where they stood. But them? Somehow, they made it out alive. And from that moment forward, every year on the anniversary of that Alive Day, they would stop whatever they were doing and celebrate the fact that although they were affected, impacted, marked, wounded, and undeniably harmed by the travesties of war, they were not dead but *alive*.

When I'd first met J. R. Martinez, I noticed a tattoo of a watch face on his wrist that I'd later learn had been "set" to the exact hour when he had been injured but didn't die. Underneath it was a tattoo of the date of his Alive Day, symbols to him that while his life had been radically and irrevocably changed that day, it had not been taken from him. He was compromised, yes, but he was not overcome. "Every time I see this ink," he said to me once, "I'm reminded to live the life I have."

For US Marine Corps Sergeant Kenneth Kalish, who began his military career in 2007 and was first deployed in 2009 to Iraq, signs of life were seemingly everywhere despite the immense challenges he faced. He and the black Labrador retriever he'd been assigned, a beautiful dog named Fynn, were working in tandem to seek out IEDs in Afghanistan in 2010 and had successfully spotted and removed six on the day when Kenny would step on a ten-pound IED pressure plate. The blast was instant and ferocious, causing Kenny to become a triple amputee, a mere twenty-eight days from the end of that deployment. Kenny lost his entire left arm, both legs, and in many ways his sturdiness as a person. He would suffer from anxiety disorder, thoracolumbar spine degenerative disc disease, memory loss, postconcussive syndrome, right shoulder impingement syndrome, hip impairments, tinnitus, right write tenosynovitis, urethral stenosis, testicular trauma, and multiple scars. In short, things were *bad* for Kenny. And yet the twenty-four-year-old kept on keeping on.

There were scores of reasons Kenny could have thrown in the towel, but he didn't. He learned to navigate life in a wheelchair. He practiced using a stick to knock down food items on the high shelves in his kitchen. He started surfing, fishing, paragliding, and, in an effort to apply his expert marksman skills to an entirely new target, hunting deer. When we gifted Kenny with his new home, in Cedar Hill near Dallas, kids from the local school came out to sing the National Anthem and to thank him for his service. I was touched when I saw the line of youngsters waiting to get Kenny's autograph—a real signature from a real American hero. For Kenny's part, he just smiled, and, in his "Aw, shucks" style, he simply said thanks.

Kenny Kalish, Sergeant, US Marine Corps, at his home under construction

During his brief military career, Kenny would be awarded a Purple

Heart, a Combat Action Ribbon, two Navy Unit Commendation ribbons, a Marine Corps Good Conduct Medal, two Sea Service deployment ribbons, a NATO Medal, a Global War on Terrorism Medal, an Iraq Campaign Medal with one star, and an Afghanistan Campaign Medal with one star, but I think the highest commendation for him is yet to come. Based on the resilience and optimism I see in Kenny, I believe he will stand before God someday and hear the words we all should long to hear: "Well done, good and faithful servant. Well done."

Hardly a New Thing

Once I had vocabulary to put to this idea of moving past one's devastating pain and seizing upon the good that still remains, I began to see the dynamic in lives beyond those of the wounded vets I so highly esteem. I make a point of reading my Bible every morning, and stories I'd read dozens of times before carried new weight in my heart. The apostle Paul had been plagued by some sort of a thorn in his flesh but chose to keep training up disciples and planting Christ-honoring churches anyway (see 2 Corinthians 12:6-8). Joseph was sold into slavery by his own brothers but picked forgiveness over revenge. David faced more trials and tribulations than he could probably count—including being hunted down by King Saul, who was determined to extinguish David's life—but he resolved in his heart to "wait on the Lord" and to trust God to set every wrong thing right (see Psalm 27). Job lost his kids, livestock, houses, and pretty much every other earthly possession a person could own, not to mention the faithfulness of his wife and closest friends, but he refused to stay down on the ten count. He stood back up and trusted God. And then there is Naomi, who lost her husband and two sons and was so despondent that she temporarily changed her name to "Bitter" (see Ruth 1:20-21). Astoundingly, even *she* would rise from the ashes, choosing to engage with the life of hers that was left to live.

I'd read those stories and think about how my own wife set her face toward a bright future on the heels of her cancer scare. And how valiant Daniel has been in the midst of his health struggles—his mind singularly focused on serving others, even on the days when his body won't comply. And how my mom, bless her soul, just won't give way to playing the victim, despite the vast justification she'd have in doing so.

I visited my mom once, when I'd been in the hill country for a client meeting and had a few unassigned hours before needing to return to Houston, where I lived at the time. My mother—Bettie Short is her name—lived in Sattler, a community below Canyon Lake, in a home overlooking a private section of the Guadalupe River that my sister and I helped Mom build years prior. It was as picturesque and peaceful a place as Texas had to offer, and as Mom and I settled into chairs on her back porch, where she and her poodle, Amber, spent a significant portion of her days, I said, "Mom, every time I come out here, I am amazed all over again by how pretty this view is."

"Oh, I know it," she replied as she patted my arm. "God has been so good to me. I just love it here . . . "

I remember thinking, "That's it? After all you've been through, no complaints?"

"Don't you get lonely now that Dick is gone?" I asked her, referring to her second husband, Richard Short, whom Mom had married after I was a grown man myself. Dick had served as a marine sniper during World War II, participating in most of the campaigns in the South Pacific including Guam and Guadalcanal but was close to the vest about his experiences there; we would learn only posthumously that he was a highly decorated and extremely accomplished marksman.

"I'm never lonely," Mom said. "Amber here keeps me plenty busy. Worse than raising a kid, I tell you."

A few seconds passed, and then my mother turned to me and said, "Danny, I am so proud of you. I always have been. But what you're doing now to help those families is just wonderful."

I kind of chuckled at that, thinking that even if I were in

prison for mass murder, Mom would find a way to be proud of me. "Well, you're the best inmate in there, I know!" she'd probably beam. A mother's encouragement infuses a special strength in her children, and though I've heard my own mom declare her pride in me a thousand times, I never grow tired of hearing those messages of confidence and love.

Replaying that afternoon conversation with Mom in my mind, I thought about how she had always been there for me, accepting me, loving me, and—especially during my dad's heavy-drinking days—protecting me as best she could. What's more, she never caved to despair, even though I know she lived through plenty of despairing days. She kept choosing life, each day that she found herself alive. Still today, that strong, beautiful woman chooses life.

Professor Pain

This latest turn of events involving my father has provided a prime—even if unsolicited—opportunity to do some soul searching . . . a little self-reflection, you might say. If the stats are right, I'm in my last third of life now, and the older I get, the more convinced I am that God allows painful things to show up in my life for the sole purpose of teaching me exactly what he wants me to learn. This isn't always a pleasant process, given that I don't tend to learn very well unless the teacher trying to teach me is pretty much hollering in my ear. I think we call that "stubbornness," an adjective well-suited for me. C. S. Lewis once wrote, "We can ignore even pleasure. But pain insists upon being attended to. God whispers to us in our pleasures, speaks in our conscience, but shouts in our pains: it is his megaphone to rouse a deaf world."[1] I take solace in Lewis' quote; at least I know I'm not alone.

The message in the madness this last time around, the lesson I think God wants me to learn, is that only he can scratch the "father itch" I've been trying to get at all these years. Ideally, earthly fathers are to manifest a level of selflessness and unconditional love in the lives of their wives and children such that it makes it easy for those loved ones to envision a gracious, loving heavenly Father, who longs for relationship with them. But even when that earthly father can't offer selflessness or unconditional love to his kids, those kids can learn by antithesis; they can survey the situation and say, "I'm even *more* blown away that there is a Father who accepts me wholly, loves me deeply, and never will leave my side, given the stuff I've been through with my dad. What a good God this God must be."

That's the category I'd say I've landed in—that of learning by way of contrast just what a magnificent God I serve. It has been confirmed in my mind and heart through prayer, through sitting with my own thoughts, through conversations with loved ones, and through reading my Bible. It has been uncanny to me that verses I've read eighty-two times across the years all of a sudden, upon that eighty-third reading, hit me—*bam*—right between the eyes. "How did I not see this truth before?" I always come away wondering. This is what it must mean that God's Word is "active," which is how Hebrews 4:12 refers to it.

Trust me as your Father, I have sensed God saying to me these last days and weeks. *Let me love you. Let me care for you. Let me prove to you that you are accepted and approved.* I have to tell you his input is balm to a beat-up soul. And while it doesn't completely remove the pain and disillusionment I've racked up over the course of this life, it rounds out the sharp edges that have pierced me on many a day. In my own way and with God's direction marking my steps, I feel myself coming back to life. The day you come too close to death but don't die can be your Alive Day, so many soldiers have taught me. And while mine wasn't a physical death, emotionally and relationally, I could relate. *I don't have to be defined by this pain,* I have begun telling myself. *I can choose to keep living this life I've been given to live.*

"Behold, I will do a new thing," the prophet Isaiah wrote, speaking on God's behalf. "Now it shall spring forth; Shall you not know it? I will even make a road in the wilderness and rivers in the desert" (Isaiah 43:19). How I crave that "new thing" he's up to. Newness is the very definition of life.

What a Blind Man Could See

Can I give you a picture of someone who despite tragic loss and overwhelming grief decides to take "living" to the absolute extreme? This guy's story will stick with you for years.

When we met Michael Malarsie, he was a Senior Airman in the air force, living his childhood dream of being a member of an elite military unit. That unit comprised Tactical Air Control Party (TACP) specialists and worked on the ground with marine and army units to direct air strikes. Michael was deployed in December 2009 with soldiers from the 4th Infantry Division out of Fort Carson, Colorado, and in January 2010 found himself headed for a routine patrol in a Kandahar village that had long since been deserted. Upon hearing and seeing no activity nearby, Michael and a squad of four other men crossed the bridge leading into the village and set up a fire team.

The man chosen to lead the group across the bridge was US Army Corporal Joshua Lengstorf. After clearing the bridge, Corporal Lengstorf stepped on an IED, the ensuing blast of which killed both him and the young Private First Class who was second in line. Third in line, Michael was hit in the neck and face with shrapnel and catapulted into the river. Instinctively, Michael struggled to find the water's surface but had a hard time orienting himself in the waves and quickly tired out. He would later say that as he gave up the fight, he had a sense of peace and calm overwhelm him that was unlike anything he'd ever known.

Within moments, an army medic had rushed to Michael's aid, pulling him out of the water and tending to his wounds. Michael survived because of that medic's quick, skillful work, but his quality of life would forever be changed.

The medic and another of Michael's teammates, Bradley

Michael Malarsie,
Senior Airman, US Air Force

Smith, offered to retrieve the fallen victims, but as they were carrying back the remains of Corporal Lengstorf, a second IED detonated, killing both of those men. Michael felt the pulse of the explosion, but then everything went black.

That same day in New Mexico, Michael's mom and dad arrived home from church to discover a voice-mail message asking them to call Michael's commander as soon as possible. This was the call no military parent or spouse wants to get: certainly your loved one has been killed.

"Michael is alive," Michael's commander reassured them, "but he has been severely injured."

Michael's parents readied themselves for an unplanned trip to Walter Reed Hospital and there found their son in grave pain. Docs had been unable to save Michael's vision, and in addition to going blind, Michael had suffered a broken jaw, a burst eardrum, and a fracture to his skull. A long scar ran down his neck from the shrapnel, and Michael's parents wondered how their son would fare from that day forward. As it turned out, they wouldn't wonder long; when the doctor entered Michael's room, Michael thanked him profusely for his efforts, said he was ready to dive headlong into a speedy recovery, and told everyone in the room that his sole mission now was to honor the sacrifices of his brothers in arms. Everyone watching saw loss. Grief. Trauma. Death. But Michael? All Michael saw was a new life, just waiting to be lived.

An Ending Only God Could Write

Four other families would come home from church or running errands that same Sunday morning to news that wasn't even remotely good. They would be informed that their loved ones not only had been injured but had been killed in the line of duty. One person to receive such news was Jesse Lengstorf, wife of deceased Corporal Joshua Lengstorf.

On that Sunday morning, she was busy buckling her young daughter into the truck so they could go for a hike with Jesse's mom. Jesse's mom came around to the driveway and told Jesse that two men were at the front door asking for her. The men were wearing military dress uniforms, which explained the concerned expression Jesse's mom wore.

Despite several requests for Jesse to step inside her home and have a seat, Jesse stood planted there on her front porch, knowing exactly what the men were going to say. "I was so numb, I couldn't cry," Jesse would later say of her reaction to their declaration—"Mrs. Lengstorf, we regret to inform you that your husband, Corporal Joshua Lengstorf, has been killed in action." Jesse slid to seated position and began trembling so badly that she couldn't get her hand to sign the paperwork the men needed signed.

Days later, she would find herself standing on the tarmac at Dover Air Force Base in Delaware on a freezing-cold January night, watching as her husband's flag-draped transfer case was unloaded from the plane. He was the first one to be presented, given his high ranking among his squad, and as the lights of the vehicle that carried his body faded into the distance, Jesse fainted into the arms of an officer standing nearby.

Simultaneously, Michael Malarsie was undergoing intense therapy sessions at the Western Blind Rehabilitation Center in Palo Alto, California, where he had been transferred following his discharge from Walter Reed. Bradley Smith's widow, Tiffany, had visited Michael while he was at Walter Reed and later had the occasion to meet Jesse as well. Michael had been blogging about the whole experience, Tiffany told Jesse, which prompted Jesse to go online and read those entries, one by one. "I kept getting this distinct impression that I needed to meet Michael," Jesse later told me. It was a nagging sense that persisted for weeks, and so finally, Jesse reached out to Tiffany and requested a meeting with Michael. Soon thereafter, Jesse and her eighteen-month-old daughter boarded a plane bound for California.

What happened next is the stuff movies are made of. Jesse and Michael exchanged a friendly hug upon meeting, swapped stories about military life and about Josh, Jesse's husband who had been killed that fateful day. "He was an amazing leader," Michael told Jesse, confirming what she already knew in her heart. Josh had been a hero to all who knew him, it seemed, his wife certainly among them.

Jesse extended her California stay in order to get to know Michael better, and despite the fact that she was a young widow still grieving the loss of her beloved husband, she couldn't deny that she was starting to feel something more than friendship for Michael Malarsie.

Michael himself had not been looking for love either, but he felt the connection too. One humorous aside is that the week just before Jesse's visit, Michael had lamented to his mom that women were going to have to come to him now, given that he couldn't see them and thus approach them to ask them out. His mom, in response, said, "Your chances aren't good of that, honey."

Little did Mom know!

After that initial visit, Jesse flew from Oregon to California nearly every week, in order to spend time getting to know Michael. Within a matter of months, both Michael and Jesse could read the proverbial writing on the wall: this relationship was heading toward permanence . . . and *fast*.

"We talked to our families," Jesse later explained, "and all of us prayed about what was happening. A short while later, we all agreed that this was the right thing."

Days before Michael returned home to New Mexico, Jesse and her daughter relocated to Albuquerque, in order to live with Michael's sister and her family. It would position her closer to Michael and allow the couple to see if a future together was really best for them. When Michael and his mom arrived home from

California, Jesse watched as Michael's dad and sisters went through the airport-security line, intending to hang back and give the family some time and space to reunite. But after hugging his immediate family and exchanging quick greetings, it was obvious to everyone there that Michael was searching for Jesse. Jesse stepped forward and began crying before she even reached Michael's arms. Michael hugged her briefly but then pulled away, which confused Jesse. As he fell to one knee, he pulled a small box from the breast pocket of his dress blues and asked Jesse to marry him then and there.

Six weeks later, Jesse and Michael exchanged their I dos; ten months later, they welcomed their baby girl, Sophie Raine, into the world. Just after celebrating their first anniversary, they relocated to Lackland Air Force Base in San Antonio so Michael could further his career in the air force. Today, he serves as the administrator for the Recovering Airman Mentorship Program, training wounded or ill airmen to be mentors to those who have just begun their recovery process and has the distinction of being the only blind airman ever to serve active duty in the US Air Force.

Even as I recount that story here for you, a tale I know so well, I am moved once again by the twists and turns it reveals. A service-oriented man witnesses the loss of his friend and brother in military action; a tender, loving widow works through her loss and ensuing emptiness—one is blinded by battle, the other blinded by pain. And yet despite all that they could not see—about the reasons for their loss, about their present circumstances, and about what the future would hold—they could see in plain view that they loved each other. Some call that fate or destiny. I call it God.

I also credit God as the creative conduit behind my team at Operation FINALLY HOME meeting the Malarsies to begin with and also behind our ability to provide them a new home. Our friend and builder Eddie Martin with Tilson Homes, who by then had already built homes for two injured veterans, agreed to manage construction, donate all labor and materials, and produce what in the end was a truly magnificent home. I catch myself from time to time replaying that scene when we surprised Jesse and Michael with the news of their new house. Jesse, awash in complete shock, looked at her husband with tears in her eyes and melted into his chest. Such a massive burden, instantaneously removed from their lives.

Current statistics say that between eighteen and twenty-two wounded veterans commit suicide each day, which equates on the high end to nearly one person an hour choosing not life but death.[2] I look at Michael—and at so many other wounded veterans I now call friends—and see with fresh perspective that regardless of how difficult life becomes, as long as we're still taking in oxygen, the option before us all is to choose life. We can choose to stay alive emotionally, to stay alive relationally, to stay alive financially, and to stay alive spiritually. In *every* regard, we can declare today an Alive Day, as long as we're still alive.

Leave a Legacy You Love

Spend a few minutes thinking through the following themes, based on the situations and stories from chapter 9:

1. What did you make of the examples of soldiers who instead of lamenting their tragic circumstances focused their attention on the fact that they'd made it out of their near-death situation alive?

2. If you could declare an Alive Day in your own life, what serious situation would you link it to and why?

3. Has God ever "spoken" to you through a painful situation? Why is pain sometimes the most fitting of all megaphones for God to use, in getting our attention?

4. In light of whatever challenges you face today, even now, what might God be trying to convey?

10

BETTER TOGETHER

EDDIE MARTIN, THE builder on the Malarsie house, exemplified the sort of can-do spirit my team and I have been spoiled with in the key partners we've worked with along the way. One of the builds he'd helped us on previously was for one of the two *Extreme Makeover: Home Edition* projects we've been part of, this one in Salado, Texas. The day of the build was upon us before we knew it, and I distinctly recall Eddie organizing his company's crews such that when the thousand women and men from Tilson who'd logged ten or twelve hours during the day were headed home for some much-needed rest, a fresh batch of energized workers were already descending on the site. What's more, he proved masterful as a leader and communicator, coordinating subcontractors, employees, volunteers, and hundreds upon hundreds of gawking onlookers who all were eager to have a look. Building a home in nine months is one thing; building one in one hundred hours? Quite another. Still, Eddie pulled it off. And he did so with precision and grace.

As I say, those of us who work inside Operation FINALLY HOME can point not only to one partner of this sort but to *dozens* of them. I've told you about our relationship to J. R. Martinez, to Kid Rock and LeAnn Rimes, and, truly, the complete list of the companies and people who have linked arms with us to pull off what has seemed impossible on many occasions would throw this book into the "doorstop" category. But some of the stories simply must be told, not to glorify those wonderful partners, and certainly not to glorify ourselves. I offer them as a means for glorifying God, the one who invented partnership to begin with.

The Beauty of Unity

The apostle Paul one time was trying to explain to some people at a church in a place called Galatia that because of Jesus' great sacrifice and great love, all of the dividing lines that had once been drawn could now officially be erased. "There is neither Jew nor Greek," he said, "there is neither slave nor free, there is neither male nor female; for you are all one in Christ Jesus" (Galatians 3:28). What this meant for those first-century believers was that all the categorization they were accustomed to doing when they met people had been made null and void. Unity was the new goal.

What Paul was echoing was the timeless priority of banding together in a noble endeavor instead of choosing to go it alone—timeless because God himself upheld it long before time existed. At the creation scene noted in Genesis, as you'll recall, when God got to the crown of creation—humankind—the pronoun used was not "I" but "we" (see Genesis 1:26). When the stakes were highest, his holy Trinity was enlisted, modeling for all future generations that we really are better together than apart. It really is good and pleasant when we "dwell together in unity," as the psalmist wrote in Psalm 133:1.

Paul would carry this theme of unity throughout his writings, encouraging us to "bear each other's burdens" (Galatians 6:2) and to "uphold the weak" (1 Thessalonians 5:14) and to be "of one accord" (Philippians 2:2), and while Lone Ranger types may find these exhortations troublesome, as it relates to Operation

FINALLY HOME, unity for me has been a breeze. I can think of at least two reasons why. For starters, I care deeply about the end game of putting deserving families into mortgage-free homes, and despite all the things I do not know, one thing I'm sure of is that there is no chance whatsoever that goal gets accomplished if I am working to accomplish it alone. *Zero* chance. *Nada. Zilch.* From day one, if any honest, reputable man, woman, or organization wanted to join me in the quest to care for our wounded veterans in this way, my answer was, "You're in." Why? Because when the stakes are highest, a team shines brightest. We're better together than apart.

But there's a second reason I find unity to be a breeze instead of a burden, which is that I am a master delegator. Some people call it laziness, but those are generally the ones who burn out early in life, exhausted from carrying the weight of the world on their own. Delegation says, *There are all these able-minded, able-bodied folks in front of me. Why not put them to work?*

At our church many years ago, one of the pastors got up on a Sunday morning and said that we needed to freshen up the sets of our "Bethlehem City" drive-through Christmas experience. Each December, we would erect various scenes depicting the birth of Jesus, and as long lines of cars snaked their way through the exhibit, passengers could tune their radio to a certain station and hear an audio recording of the Christmas story that coincided with each of those scenes. The pastor cited a date and time when volunteers could come to the church and help rebuild, repair, or repaint the scenes, and I logged the information away, thinking it was something I'd like to do.

Well, I arrived at that volunteer meeting, along with about sixty other tool-belt-wearing, tool-wielding guys, and after ten minutes of wandering around, watching grown men stuff their faces with donuts, I was ready to get to work. Since nobody else took charge, I took it upon myself to speak up. "Good morning, everyone!" I hollered about the quiet roar of banter. "If you're a building foreman, head to that corner. Painters? This corner. Designers? You all convene in the middle of the room." Within five minutes, I had five dozen people organized into crews, appointed crew foremen over each one, and was knocking out the task at hand. Five hours later, those sets were flawless. We saved Christmas that day, the lot of us! See what a little "laziness" can do?

As Operation FINALLY HOME got underway and began adding staff to our team, I probably sounded like a broken record. We'd make a hire. I'd sit down with the person who just came aboard, and I'd deliver my typical spiel: "I don't micromanage. Here is the job you have been hired to do. Here is the goal we're chasing. Go forth and prosper, my friend." We are up to twelve employees now, and I am convinced that collectively we do the work of forty or forty-five people. Why? Because we are unified under the banner of a common, compelling objective. We're in this thing together, not to control one another, but to spur one another to love and good deeds, as Scripture says (Hebrews 10:24). God has brought us together, God has given us a big assignment, and just as Carol said he would, God has equipped us with every resource necessary to do what he's called us to do—and then some. So far, in just our first eleven years, one hundred homes have built for one hundred worthy families, and based on today's in-progress builds and what's slated for the months to come, the next hundred will be completed by 2018. *That's* the beauty of unity. We're better together than apart.

Partner Number One

In many ways, every good partnership that has emerged for Operation FINALLY HOME can be traced back to our first partner in crime, the Cable News Network. It was their *Heroes* show that put us on the national map, so to speak, which to this gun-owning, Bush-supporting, ranch-living Texas cowboy was a real shock. First of all, I knew that tens of thousands of people from all over the world are nominated each year; how on earth did my tiny group stand a chance? And second, as everybody knows, God watches Fox News not CNN. If he was going to bless me through some national media channel, it certainly wouldn't be this one.

Boy, was I put in my place—which is a key takeaway for me as it relates to partnership: You just never know who God will bring your way. I would come to find out that the people working at all levels over at CNN are smart, savvy, and respectful women and men who, to a person, have hearts as big as Texas. They could have eyed me with the same level of skepticism that I was eyeing them, but they didn't. They welcomed me in, treated me with dignity and professionalism, asked insightful questions, honored the wounded vets I deeply love, and in the end, a few of them even became friends. Who would have thought this was possible? Certainly not me.

CNN's stamp of approval—if I can call it that—catapulted Operation FINALLY HOME to a totally different level, and it happened nearly overnight. I've mentioned the relationship we established with one of the divisional presidents of PulteGroup, as of 2015 the third largest homebuilder in the country. This operation is *huge*, and for reasons only God himself knows, they wanted to join forces with *us*. What happened was that we needed to build a home in Fort Worth, Texas, for Jason Vest and his family, and we needed to do it fast. Jason was a captain in the air force who as a Special Forces pilot had flown many missions, both for the Operation Enduring Freedom and for the Operation Iraqi Freedom campaigns. Most of those flights took place over burning oil fields and burn pits, and as a result of Jason's exposure to the gases, he contracted Lambert-Eaton Myasthenia Syndrome, a rare neuromuscular disease. Because the VA hospital could not definitively identify the origin of Jason's problem, they were unable to provide with any confidence a worthwhile treatment protocol. Jason's immune system began attacking his own body, and doctors feared the worst. One oncologist told Jason's wife that if further tests didn't reveal the origin of Jason's disease, he would most certainly die—news that was especially devastating to the couple's two young kids.

The day that Jason was medically discharged from the military and informed that his pay would henceforth be cut in half, Daniel reached out to Pulte's Fort Worth office—the local guys—and told them what we were up against. They'd heard about our work from the coverage we received following the CNN *Heroes* show, and so when Daniel told them we didn't know where else to turn, they graciously said in response, "Let's meet."

These divisional offices of Pulte are run autonomously for the most part, as long as they are profitable, and so the decision had come quickly and easily—just like that, they were in, not just for the build, but for the lot as well.

Pulte and Operation FINALLY HOME linked arms, built the Vests' home, and felt deep-seated gratitude upon being able to hand over those house keys to a family so in need.

After that build, in a grassroots ripple effect similar to the one we experienced with LP Building Products, the presidents of all the Pulte divisional offices convened for their annual meeting and started swapping stories about what they'd been up to. The Fort Worth team evidently bragged on their work with Operation

Jason Vest, Captain, US Air Force, and family

FINALLY HOME, which caught the other heads' attention. By the time the meeting dismissed, I had a message on my phone to call the CEO of PulteGroup. "You need to come up here and talk to us," he said. "My guys love you!"

After we convened with both the company's CEO and the CFO and told them our story, they decided to endorse partnership with Operation FINALLY HOME from the top down. It's a good thing Daniel and I were seated, because I doubt our legs could have held us upon hearing that incredible news.

Publicity We Couldn't Buy

As if CNN hadn't already done enough to elevate the public's awareness of our work, three years after the *Heroes* show aired, one of their producers called to tell me that the network wanted to do an hour-long follow-up special on Operation FINALLY HOME. The show wasn't going to be about war, mind you, or about terrorism or about wounded veterans in general. It was going to be about Operation FINALLY HOME's work—specifically. My mind whirred. "Are you serious?" I asked the producer, to which he said, "Yes, sir. Totally."

We would never in a million years be able to afford publicity like this, and yet we'd never have to. It was being handed to us, free of charge.

As soon as the producer netted out the goal for the show, which was to trail a couple of wounded veterans and their families for a few days and show their living conditions and how these mortgage-free homes blessed them, I knew exactly who should be featured. Daniel had been in contact with a VA caseworker at Brooke Army Medical Center in San Antonio about a family who had some serious needs. US Army Sergeant Stephen Jackel joined the military in 2008 and soon thereafter was deployed to Iraq and then Afghanistan, where he would provide such stellar service that he would be awarded the Purple Heart, among other honors. But his tenure would not be without its devastating effects; on

August 23, 2011, while on convoy with his team in an RG-31, a steel-welded mine-resistant vehicle equipped with a roof-mounted gun station, Stephen would notice a wire running into the culvert they'd approached several seconds too late. An IED had been initiated, the blast of which would lift that massive vehicle off the ground and knock Stephen unconscious.

When Stephen came to, he realized that in addition to his legs having been utterly crushed, he was now trapped inside the burning vehicle along with his team members. He remembers the finality of the moment, believing with every certainty that this was where—and how—he would die.

Just then, a rush of heat flooded the vehicle and compelled Stephen to act. He grabbed his leg and began slamming it in every direction in order to put out the fires surrounding him and then used the little strength he had left to lift his broken body up and out of the vehicle's top hatch. Once out, he turned and assisted the rest of his team to safety. Moments later, shredded from the experience, Stephen collapsed.

The blast would leave Stephen with severe injuries, including bilateral below-the-knee amputations and a traumatic brain injury. He also received multiple soft-tissue injuries from shrapnel and would fall into depression as a result of his pain. What's more, upon returning home, Stephen's injuries would sideline him from revenue-producing activity, which meant he could not afford housing for his wife and their six kids.

I wanted the Jackels in a house, and I wanted the whole thing captured by CNN for the entire world to see. Daniel and I started scheming toward that end.

Big, Huge Talent; Itty-Bitty Ego

Around the time that all of this was unfolding, we were busy hosting an event at Fair Park, site of the annual State Fair of Texas. Featured artists included legendary country singer Kix

Brooks, of the duo Brooks and Dunn. We'd met Kix sometime prior, after Daniel did a radio interview with him for his show *American Country Countdown*, and so we asked him if he wanted to be in on our big plan.

Soon enough, Carol and I were loading up with the rest of the Operation FINALLY HOME crew, driving to the Dallas fairgrounds, and anticipating great things as the Jackels learned of their new home. And we were doing all of it with CNN videographers in tow.

Right in line with our strategy, Daniel had invited Stephen, his wife, Adriana, and their beautiful children to attend the fair. He had secured downtown hotel rooms for them so they could enjoy a weekend getaway from their cramped quarters in San Antonio and had handed them backstage passes to Kix's concert—"Just in case you guys want to meet some country royalty," Daniel had explained. Stephen graciously accepted the invitation to come and said his kids would be overjoyed to be backstage at a "real" concert.

Three songs into his set, Kix called Sergeant Jackel and his family to join him at center stage, and he introduced this true American hero to the crowd, who then cheered so wildly and loudly that Kix himself was overwhelmed. A giant rendering of

Stephen Jackel, Sergeant, US Army,
surprise at Kix Brooks and friends concert in Dallas

the Jackels' new home was then presented to the family, and the crowd cheered all over again. As we all stood there basking in the unrestrained applause for all that Stephen had sacrificed on our country's behalf, I felt like the luckiest man in the world. To get to do this type of work, with these types of selfless partners, on behalf of women and men who lay it all on the line for freedom's sake—the whole deal leaves me undone.

Kix Brooks proved to me that just because a person has huge talent, a huge platform, and is hugely famous by this world's standards, he doesn't have to have a correspondingly huge ego. In fact, time and again, I am stunned by the graciousness, the focus, the compassion, the humility, and the generosity of the superstars we're privileged to meet. You may recall the build we did for Erasmo Valles—the first build Daniel and I worked on together, in fact. He is the marine lieutenant who despite having become an amputee after his vehicle ran over an IED while in Iraq wanted to pursue his master's degree in business administration at the University of Houston.

At the time, the Valles family was still living in San Antonio, and I remember racking my brain over how to present the news of their new home to them in a memorable way. Knowing I was trolling for ideas, Daniel said, "Hey, why don't you surprise them in conjunction somehow with Ted and Shemane's dedication this summer for the pavilion?"

The "Ted" he was referring to was legendary musician Ted Nugent and his wife, Shemane, and the pavilion was a covered area they were erecting at Brooke Army Medical Center in San Antonio, so burn patients would have an outside seating area that was shielded from the direct sunlight that was so harmful to their fragile skin. It would be but one of dozens of contributions Ted has made to military servicemen and servicewomen and their families, including revitalizing children's play areas, donating spa services to military wives, and building recreational areas at various military hospitals.

Daniel had met Ted at an event for wounded troops at Billy Bob's, the legendary Fort Worth concert hall, and later escorted Ted and his family on a tour of Brooke Army Medical Center, where the singer would play acoustic guitar for groups of amputees upon request and would voluntarily scrub in and suit up in a sterile gown, cap, gloves, and mask, in order to gain access to the unit housing the most severe burn patients. Daniel recalls seeing Ted emerge from the room of one soldier who had sustained burns to more than 90 percent of his body. The star had entered the room with his guitar but had left empty-handed. Daniel knew full well what had happened; after playing a few songs for the young man who was fully strapped to his hospital bed, lest even a tiny, accidental movement tear his skin prematurely, he'd handed his beloved instrument to the soldier's mother, who had yet to leave her boy's side. Outside the room, Ted Nugent wept. He then hugged his son, Rocco, who had accompanied him on the visit, a little tighter. "What you just saw today was the price of freedom," he would later say to Rocco, wiping tears from the edge of his eyes.

Presenting the Valleses with their home during the dedication of that patio was a fantastic idea, and Ted was all too eager to participate. It went off without a hitch and was a star-studded event, thanks to the kindness of a rock star who considers others' needs above his own.

Good Causes Attract Good People

A final thought, as it relates to joining with others in pursuit of the mission God gives us, rather than opting for independence, which in the end only glorifies self: If the last ten years have taught me anything, it's that if I'm careful to devote myself to a good cause, my efforts will attract good people. I've seen this dynamic too many times for it to be coincidence. I don't have to go seek out people to work with; all I have to do is stay laser focused on my good calling, and God will rally good people to my side.

It happened that way with Daniel, J.R., and Kid Rock. It

happened that way with Ted Nugent, LeAnn Rimes, and Kix
Brooks. It happened that way with LP Building Products, which,
I must mention, is where we found Rusty Carroll, the man who
so readily caught our vision upon first meeting Daniel and me
barely a year after he left his senior-level position in an industry
he'd served for a full twenty years. He came aboard with Operation FINALLY HOME and proceeded to overwhelm our entire
system with brilliant insights, useful connections, and enthusiasm that still hasn't waned.

It happened that way with the PulteGroup. It happened
that way with the scores of vendors, who donate such staggering
quantities of materials that it would put even the world's greatest
philanthropists to shame. It happened that way with JC Pen-
ney, who is now a supporter of ours. It happened that way with
Southern Living magazine's Southern Living Custom Builder
Program, who just recently declared us their charity of choice and
with whom we partner on several builds a year. It happened that
way with Gateway Church in Southlake, Texas, whose members
banded together in raising tens of thousands of dollars to sponsor
a new home. It happened that way with HEB, the $23 billion
grocery-store chain that decided to involve us in their annual
Tournament of Champions, during which the sixteen hundred
CEOs from HEB's principal suppliers—Nestlé, Coca Cola,
Frito Lay, General Mills, Folgers, to name a few—convene in
San Antonio, Texas, for a full day of volunteerism, which now
involves landscaping our most recent builds.

It happens that way with individual sponsors, who pony up
initial funding for these houses. It happens that way with throngs
of neighbors who haul out barbecue grills and create entire parade
routes in order to celebrate a wounded veteran's new home. It happens that way with small-business owners who happen to be at
those home-dedication events and come up to me afterward to
say, "I will donate housecleaning to this family every month they
call this place home"; "I have a landscaping business. You tell the

owners their yard is taken care of"; or "I do snow plowing for a few businesses around here. Tell them not to buy a shovel."

And, to my eternal surprise, it even happens that way with professional sports teams who, on several occasions already, have actually asked if they can sponsor us. In their business model, that's unheard of. Thankfully, it's not unheard of in God's.

The Result of Togetherness

To substantiate the wild claim I've just made, let me let you peek at one of the NFL builds we've enjoyed along the way. The family in need belonged to Fort Polk, Louisiana-based US Marine Corps Staff Sergeant Scott Wood, who had completed two tours in Iraq and one in Afghanistan. During his last two deployments, Scott sustained several injuries from an IED explosion, resulting in a concussion and a contusion on his head. Additionally, he suffered from TBI and PTSD and was in need of several surgeries for his back.

When Scott's wife, Sarah, realized that Scott's meds were not alleviating his intense daily pain, she tried desperately to have him admitted at Brooke Army Medical Center in San Antonio, which would involve a transfer from the hospital in Louisiana, where Scott was a patient. In the midst of that fight, the couple learned that Scott had received a furlough from the hospital to go home for Thanksgiving, and so, figuring the break might have a cathartic effect on Scott, they packed up and headed for Alvin, Texas, where Sarah's parents live.

Back in Alvin, Scott and his three-year-old son, Landon, played soccer in the front yard and wrestled on the living room floor, a signal to Sarah and her parents that maybe Scott was getting better after all. "We could get used to this quality of life!" Sarah remembers thinking, just before the bottom of that life fell out.

The next morning, a Saturday, Landon wandered into the living room, where his dad was napping on the couch. His mom had told him that Scott was tired and needed to catch up on his sleep, but Landon couldn't contain his excitement over wanting to play with his dad. "Daddy!" he whispered, a giant grin on his face. "Daddy!" But Scott didn't stir. Landon upped the ante by patting his dad's shoulder, but still: nothing. He then fiddled with his dad's fingers and shook his dad's arm, but nothing was working. His dad wouldn't move.

Moments later, Sarah entered the room and instinctively knew. Her beloved had died in his sleep.

When Daniel got wind of this family's tragic situation, he called me and said, "We need to approve them for a home . . . and *now*." Within days, we had a lot pinpointed and a builder selected, but still, there was no sponsor to be found. And then my phone rang. We'd been in conversation with the Houston Texans, specifically about this build, and now they wanted in.

Daniel and I took the first available meeting slot the Texans' marketing head offered us and zipped over to tell his team Sarah and Landon's story. Would we want to surprise Sarah at an upcoming game? They asked us. We told them we loved the idea, and that was before we knew Sarah was a raving Texans fan. She would later tell us that her husband was so devoted to the team that back when he had told Sarah of his wishes, should he ever meet an untimely demise, he insisted on being buried in his marine dress blues . . . with his Andre Johnson jersey underneath.

It was a sell-out crowd at Reliant Stadium the night that Sarah and Landon took to the stands. We'd told them that the Texans were giving out Christmas presents to deserving children at the end of the first quarter and that they had been selected to take part. This was, in fact, the truth, given that Landon received a bundle of amazing new toys that night, including his first "real" bike. But it wasn't the *whole* truth, as Sarah was about to find out. After an announcer had told the audience about Scott's ordeal and about Sarah and Landon's attendance at the game, he said, "And Sarah, Landon isn't the only one getting gifts here tonight. The Houston Texans are proud to partner with Operation FINALLY HOME to build you and Landon a brand-new mortgage-free house in your hometown of Alvin, Texas."

With that, Sarah turned toward me, buried her head in my chest, and cried uncontrollably. My smile was so big that I thought my cheeks might burst from all the pressure. I couldn't bring Scott back for her. But at least I could be part of a plan that would give her a sense of security, a sense of being protected, and a sense of being *home*. As the stadium crowd jumped to their feet, whooping, hollering, and applauding, little Landon looked at me with an expression that said, *What in the world is going on?*

I tussled the hair on his head and said, "Someday, this will all make sense to you, little guy. For now, just know that your mama's as happy as she's able to be."

On the day of the Woods' home dedication, the tangle of excited neighbors was flanked by Houston Texan players and cheerleaders, who had come out on their own time to wish Sarah well. As she gently closed her new front door on the party going on outside, wanting just for a few moments to roam through her new home alone, she happened upon a bonus room we'd built for her, a small sitting area off to the side. We'd decorated it with all of Scott's marine gear, including a shadow box containing the Purple Heart he'd received. She ran her fingers along the edge of the frame and said, "Now this place feels like home."

I'm telling you, nothing beats the feeling of helping a person

Sarah Woods (far right), widow of US Marine Corps Staff Sergeant Scott Woods, surprised at Houston Texans game

feel whole. I know it. Our Operation FINALLY HOME partners know it. And in your heart of hearts, I bet you know it too. We owe it to one another to stick together in life because big dreams only get accomplished by big cooperation—us with God and also us with one another. Jesus and his early followers had it exactly right: This unity thing is the X factor, and without it, we'll all fall down. But with it? Oh, how we'll prevail. We will defy human logic. We will render impotent balance sheets. We will be reminded of the bigger picture. And we will change this world for good.

Leave a Legacy You Love

Spend a few minutes thinking through the following themes, based on the situations and stories from chapter 10:

1. If isolation and integration are two ends of the same social-preference spectrum, which end do you tend to move toward most often, that of being ultraindependent or that of being surrounded on all sides by trusted friends? How have you come to the preference you give way to here?

2. Do you agree or disagree with the statement, "When the stakes are highest, a team shines brightest. We're better together than apart." Why?

3. How would you rate yourself in terms of being good at inviting others to participate in your life and in terms of delegating to other gifted people those tasks and roles you aren't so good at accomplishing?

4. In the same way that I "fessed up to having errantly prejudged those working at CNN," whom have you kept at arm's length along the way, only to later realize that

the person/group/organization was not at all what you imagined them to be?

5. In your view, who would be the most shocking person or group for God to bring into your life for the sole purpose of accomplishing the mission or calling he has in store for you? Why would it be such a shock? How do you think you'd respond? Consider asking God to prepare you even now, to have an open mind, an open heart, and wide-open arms that can receive the comrades he plans to send your way.

WHY WE DO
WHAT WE DO

I INTRODUCED YOU to Monte Bernardo previously, the army staff sergeant who lost his right arm and both his legs when he accidentally sat down on a bomb while serving a tour of duty in Afghanistan. As I said, my colleagues and I knew we wanted to build Monte a home so he could fulfill his dream of finding employment and financially supporting his daughter. Specifically, Monte wanted to enroll at Texas A&M University in College Station, Texas, to study engineering, and so, to College Station we would go.

Daniel and I learned of a quaint neighborhood ten miles outside of town that was filled with sprawling one-acre lots, in an area that was quiet and pastoral, even as there was a Walmart eight minutes away. The best news of all? A developer we'd been in touch with had offered it to us for free. "It's perfect," Daniel said, catching my eye, to which I nodded and with a grateful heart said, "Yep."

We set to work, building the best possible home we could build for Monte, anticipating with each step of the process his thriving in his new place.

Notes of Love

Partway through the Bernardo build, as was the case with every build we'd ever commenced, we halted production for an entire day so that builders, suppliers, decorators, and members of the community could come participate in what we call Notes of Love.

With each Operation FINALLY HOME build, there are essentially five key events: It all begins with a town hall meeting, where a builder who has raised his hand and said, "I want to be involved" convenes with every subcontractor, supplier, and business partner he knows for the purpose of hearing the story of the soldier for whom the home is being built and pledging time, money, or materials toward the build. A rep from Operation FINALLY HOME—either one of my staff or me—is generally the one telling the story, and nine times out of ten, we barely get to the end of our prepared remarks before some electrician pipes up with, "I'll wire the whole thing for free," or some lumber-yard owner says, "The studs and rafters are on me."

It's a beautiful sight to behold.

Following the town hall meeting, the builder tallies all of the pledges received and lays out a budget. To give you a general sense for what the numbers look like, the average value of the homes we build is right at three hundred grand, and the average amount we need to raise in order to build them is less than $75,000. See? I told you the building community is generous!

The second of the five key events is the surprise, and as I've alluded to, we have pulled off surprises at concerts, sporting events, family reunions, Christmas parties, and more. Once we have taken pains to vet a family—by looking into their criminal background, their financial stability (it may sound strange, but you have to be able to afford a free home), their marital and parenting "all-rightness," and the soldier's reputation among military leaders—we are eager to point all of our energies toward honoring the family, blessing the family, and providing something special for the family. And it all starts with the surprise. It never gets old, seeing the shocked expression on the faces of such deserving souls, when that announcement is made: "You are the recipient of a custom mortgage-free home!"

Ahhh. The feeling is like nothing you can imagine.

The third and fifth events are the groundbreaking and the home dedication, and because every developer we've ever worked with is overjoyed when he realizes he is going to have a military hero in one of his communities, we use these events as a way to share that joy. On both occasions, we invite neighbors, the media, and the family themselves to the site, and in my experience, two things are always true: people come in droves, and they go with tears in their eyes.

Between those two happenings, of course, is the magical day we set aside for the event known as Notes of Love. Once a home has reached dry-in status and is ready for insulation, we stop everything; we rally partners, sponsors, and the community at large; we pass out permanent markers; and we tag the studs with notes of love. The family is intentionally "locked out" of their own home for that entire day, so that once the final note has been written they can roam through slowly, quietly, and by themselves, taking in the sentiments one by one:

Season everything with love. Welcome home!

Thank you for your service and sacrifice. May you make beautiful memories here at home.

God bless you for your selflessness. We are free because of you.

I pray your days here are blessed.

From my heart to yours, thank you.

May this home be a new beginning for you. We can never repay our debt to you for your service to our country. You are loved.

May your family feel protected every day. Thank you for protecting mine.

Stopping production during a build is a terribly inefficient thing to do, and yet giving people an opportunity to express their support, to write out their prayers, and to convey to those wounded vets that others are rooting for them to thrive has proven to be a critical part of each project's plan. On too many occasions to count, families have told me that after being in their new house for weeks or even months, they would come home after a long day and be so overwhelmed by feelings of love and peace that seemed to emanate from the walls surrounding them that they would fall to their knees in awe. The words of encouragement and gratitude minister to the families to whom they are written long after they've been covered by plaster and paint.

The Importance of Coming Home

On November 17, 2012, Operation FINALLY HOME invited Monte Bernardo and his girlfriend and family to the Texas A&M Military Appreciation Game, where he would be honored for his service. He was standing midfield accepting a game football during halftime to the roar of one hundred thousand screaming fans, when on the Jumbotrons appeared Texas Governor Rick Perry to announce that Monte was our latest recipient of a custom-built home. The look on Monte's face was priceless— pure shock, pure joy, and total relief. His quivering jaw told me all I needed to know, and as I took in the sight of his girlfriend and family with tears streaming down their faces, I was reminded afresh of why we do what we do.

For many decades now, I have been intrigued by what happens when a person sets foot in his or her new home. There is such pride there, such a sense of accomplishment, such an overwhelming and all-consuming joy. When I owned my homebuilding business, I devoted an inordinate amount of attention to learning exactly what my clients needed and wanted in a home. I engaged them in multiple one-on-one interviews to learn how they planned to use each room, how the sun would strike those rooms during various times of day, how they felt about this shade of paint or that, and seemingly a thousand things more.

During walkthroughs with my clients—this would have been after the house was completed and I was about to turn over the key—I would notice the most miniscule errors, such as an inch of jaggedness on a corner paint line or uneven finish in a wall's texture or a baseboard nail that wasn't flush—things the client never would have noticed in a million years—and because I'd become so invested in the process of providing just the right place that created just the right feeling for that client, I'd be compelled to get those errors fixed. This was their *home*—the place where they would spend the vast majority of their time, the space they would call their own, and the environment they'd come to wear like a favorite sweatshirt. I wanted it to be utterly right.

While building someone a home fulfills a very basic need—shelter—there is more to why we do what we do than helping meet people's physiological needs. I've always believed that our desire to not just *be* home but also to *feel* at home is a longing given to us by God and therefore runs deep—soulishly deep. And for too many of the women and men who join the military, the economic depression and prevailing sense of hopelessness that oppressed them every day of their growing-up years meant they never once had that soulish craving fulfilled. Sometimes there was alcohol abuse. Sometimes Mom or Dad's escapism involved drugs. In many cases, their parents divorced, leaving one or the other to frantically play both roles. Money was tight, predictability came at a premium, and pressure was always sky-high. But then along came military involvement and with it an opportunity to start fresh. At last, they knew what was expected of them. At last, they knew how to succeed. At last, they had some semblance of family. At last, they'd found their way *home*.

And so they signed up.

And they trained.

And they deployed.

And they fought.

But then seemingly out of nowhere, Humvees rolled forward, IEDs exploded, limbs went flailing, and consciousness was lost.

And they came back wounded.

Shocked.

Impaired.

Facing a future shrouded in the unpredictability they so despised.

The family they'd made for themselves was fractured. The routine they'd prized was gone. The peace that comes with knowing how to thrive went missing, and once again, they longed for home.

If I've seen this progression once, I've seen it a hundred times. The valiant warriors who lay it all on the line in defense of our freedom return to this country homeless and hurt. The houses they lived in can no longer accommodate their needs, and they can't afford anything that will. They turn to their parents and siblings, but sometimes the dysfunction they originally tried to escape from prevents those family members from providing any real sense of aid. And so they're left without shelter, without meaningful work, and without anyone who will stand by their side.

Monte Bernardo's neighbors in King Oaks, the neighborhood outside of College Station where his home had been built, were so excited about welcoming a bona fide war hero into their community that in his honor they staged a full-on city-wide parade. As Monte drove up to his house that first time, he was escorted all the way down the street by twelve veterans on Harleys, and despite the loud rumbling of those amazing engines, the crowd's collective roar was louder still. Men, women, and children lined the road on both sides, waving miniature American flags and clapping their hands, and somebody had even assembling a classic-rock garage band that blared crowd-pleasing tunes for well over an hour. One neighbor had set up his barbecue pit, complete with folding dining tables dotting his driveway and yard, and before and during all of the home-dedication festivities, delighted attenders chomped down on burgers and brats.

As the prized house key was handed over to Monte, the already loud cheering became thunderous in tone. Through broken syllables and choked-up coughing, Monte said, "I don't consider myself a hero, but you've made me feel like one today." As he brushed his arm across his teary eyes, he said, "All I can do is thank you all, for everything you have done. You keep saying there's no way you can repay me for my contribution . . . the truth is, I can't repay you for yours."

Stealing away from the crowd for a few moments so he could wander through his new home alone, Monte hobbled his way through his brand-new front door, tears springing again to his eyes. As he gently shut the door behind him, I stood there on his front lawn, a whole swarm of loving friends and neighbors surrounding me, thinking, *This is why we do what we do.*

In his book, *Home: How Habitat Made Us Human,* John Allen wrote, "Home is not simply a location on the landscape where a person lives . . . Home provides a place for human beings to prepare to face the outside world."[1] When Monte reemerged from the tour of his new house, the smile that had taken over his face was the biggest I'd ever seen him wear. The world he'd returned to after his latest tour had proven more than a little tough to take. But here, now, with this instant support system flanking him, all I could do was shake my head in gratitude and say silently, *You're going to do great, Monte. Just great.*

For so many other soldiers we've encountered, the prospects weren't nearly as good.

A Needed Slice of Peace

I mentioned earlier that Operation FINALLY HOME participated in not one but two builds with *Extreme Makeover: Home Edition,* and that second one took place in Ottawa, a town near Kansas City, Kansas. The home was for US Army Staff Sergeant

Allen Hill, his wife, Gina, and their two young sons. Allen was nearly killed by a roadside bomb during his second deployment to Iraq in 2007, and although his injuries hadn't required amputation, Allen experienced a traumatic brain injury and since then had wrestled with intense and persistent PTSD symptoms.

When it comes to the struggles of our wounded veterans, it's the silent suffocator, this awfulness known as PTSD. If you go to war and come home missing a leg or an arm or large pieces of flesh that have been burned off of your body, it is obvious you are in need. Aid givers immediately know where to direct their efforts and on many occasions readily jump in. But if you go to war and come home with posttraumatic stress disorder, assistance is a little tougher to reap. If all your bodily pieces are intact, can you still be considered disabled? If your biggest problem is "all in your mind," is that really a problem at all?

If you *look* fine, aren't you fine?

More than a decade ago, an NBC News report found that one in eight returning soldiers were plagued by PTSD.[2] Based on the veterans I come across in daily life, I suspect the percentage is greater now. More troubling still was the same study's finding that more than half never seek treatment for their pain. If you're disabled, you're disabled, whether that disability is centralized in

Allen Hill, Staff Sergeant, US Army, and family

your body or brain. Part of why I was so enthusiastic about helping the Hill family was that I figured the publicity the build would undoubtedly receive might educate us all on what's true: those with PTSD need our assistance and *fast*. These soldiers' lives are quite literally on the line.

PTSD sufferers are hypertuned to their environment, needing things to be "just so," and for Allen, his needs revolved around wide hallways, large rooms, and perfect silence. We'd heard about the trauma he'd suffered in his previous home, which was situated near both a rock quarry and railroad tracks. "He didn't cope well," Gina told us, "The noises . . . they freaked him out." At unexpected hours of the day and night, Allen would hear a train blare outside, and in his mind, he was plunged back into a war scene, where he was surrounded on all sides by armed enemies. As if this wasn't enough, surveyors of the rock quarry near the subdivision ramped up excavation activity, and each time a blast sounded or a drill began cracking stone, Allen, convinced it was hostile fire, would search every room in the house, clearing them one by one of enemies, and then take cover in the corner for hours. Commercial airliners overhead could set him off. Storm sirens so common in Kansas could set him off. Even driving under a bridge while traveling along the interstate could set him off. *All* of life, it seemed, threatened him. He was struggling just to survive.

At some point, he stopped picking up his mail from the box at his driveway's end, thinking that indoors was far safer than out. And then life became so overwhelming for Allen that he refused to get out of bed. His typically gentle countenance hardened. His tone became abrupt. His attitude soured. And his adoring children dissolved into fear and insecurity, believing that whoever this man was that had replaced their kind, loving father was surely going to someday hurt them.

Gina wanted her husband back and was therefore relieved when she learned that a mental-health advocacy group had awarded Allen a Labrador retriever named Frankie, trained by prison inmates to help medically dependent owners. In no time, whenever Allen would have one of his "episodes," Frankie would jump up and lightly lick him on the face and hands. It was enough to jolt Allen back to present reality but not enough to cure him long-term.

For our part, we would wind up using glass panels to line the hallways in Allen's home, to avoid having him feel boxed in. We triple-paned his windows to keep outside noise to a whisper. We heavily insulated the walls. We also built him a "quiet room" that was freezing cold and soundproof and lightproof, so he would have a place to go when he needed to regroup. And we set the entire spread on a lovely three-acre plot of land in a small, quiet subdivision, far away from highway noise. We dotted all our *i*'s, we crossed all our *t*'s, and we made sure things were "just so." But there was only so much we could control. When the 2009 shootings happened at Fort Hood, Allen fell into such a state of despondency that he attempted suicide. Gina immediately sought out assistance from the VA, but her pleas, while impassioned, could not prompt them to action. Allen's disorder was deemed "too severe."

Allen—along with Frankie—would go on to spend a full year at a residential treatment center in California and through their interaction with group-counseling and activity-based sessions such as bowling and rock climbing would make great strides while there, but when it was time to return home to Kansas, Allen's progress seemed to fade away. He was scared to return to the very environment that had caused him so much consternation before. He hadn't been able to thrive last time; would this time prove any different?

Allen would in fact return home, and he would do his level best to stay in the present, to stay in control of his reactions, and to thrive. I wish I could tell you that everything turned around for him, that therapy and meds had worked a collective miracle, and that he was wholly happy and healthy today. But it didn't, they couldn't, and he's not. He is, however, doing *better*, and better's far better than worse.

I first met Allen at a café in the heart of Topeka, Kansas. I'd arrived early and had already been seated, when I heard a commotion at the entrance that drew my gaze. It was the Hills—Gina, Allen, Allen's service dog, Frankie—and the first impression I made of Allen was that he possessed a faraway look in his eyes. As Gina baby-stepped him into the establishment, I noticed Allen's eyes were as big as half-dollars; his gaze was directed upward, where the ceiling is met by the walls; and he kept both of his arms outstretched the entire time he walked, and his back plastered to a wall. When Gina finally reached the table where I'd been sat, her husband was in Iraq.

Frankie jumped up on Allen's chest, licking him over and over again, willing him with incessant canine syllables to come back to here, to now, but it was having little effect. "Allen!" Gina repeated over and over again. "Allen. Allen! *Hey!*"

As everyone in the café stared in our direction, Gina's pleas finally connected, and he met my eyes with a smile. "This is Mr. Wallrath, Allen," Gina said gently to him. "Allen, say hello."

Behind us, a restaurant server accidentally dropped a coffee cup, and with the crash of porcelain against tile flooring, Allen came undone. He jumped out of his seat and with arms outstretched rushed back to the safety of the wall. Frankie was right there with him, matching him stride for panicked stride, and as he stood there rubbernecking the environment, searching for the danger he felt sure was there, the dog leaped and licked and whimpered and danced, determined to bring Allen back.

"It's the most severe form of PTSD I've ever seen," Allen's psychiatrist would later declare, a statement I wouldn't find at all hard to believe. Today, despite his frequent episodes, Allen is thriving in many important ways. He is studying computer science at Ottawa University in Kansas. He is teaching his kids to play sports and ride bikes. He is working to respond quickly to Frankie. And he is determined to overcome.

I like to think that coming home to his custom-fitted house has something to do with his progress, perhaps having that slice of peace in a loud, harried world somehow gives him the fuel to survive. Of course I can't solve his PTSD or remove his memories or make him "okay." But what I can do is build him a house, wrap a loving community around him, and welcome him home.

Finally Home

Last year, some of my colleagues and I attended *Southern Living*'s national conference, this time in Nashville, Tennessee. As I mentioned, we've been partnering together, and the event gave us an excuse to give away yet another home. One of the evening's festivities included Songwriters' Night—a mini concert, if you will. Writers who put together the songs we know and love on country music radio stations took the stage to tell the stories behind their favorite lyrics, which have been made famous by Brad Paisley, Blake Shelton, Trace Adkins, and more. And then they sang those beloved tunes, causing everyone in attendance to swoon.

It was a great night, made even greater by what happened at the end. Just before I departed, songwriter Rob Crosby approached me and said, "Dan, I love what you're doing with Operation FINALLY HOME. If there's ever anything I can do for you guys, just let me know."

I thought about his offer for a second and then said, "Rob, we need a song."

My colleagues and I are always putting together videos of our work, not only so we'll have archived footage but also so our homeowners will have films to watch across the years. A *song*—an official Operation FINALLY HOME song—would be very cool to include.

A couple of months after that conference, I was checking my e-mail in my home office, when a note popped into my inbox. It was my friend Gary Henley, who happened to be one of Southern Living's certified builders, and he was forwarding a note he'd received from Rob Crosby. "Dan, have a listen," said the note, which was attached to an mp3 file. I turned up my speakers, clicked on Play, and let my spine fall into the back of my chair. "Finally Home," he'd named the song, which had me at the opening riff.

I've walked into the fire of the fight
Seen the loss and the cost of sacrifice
But after all the distant roads that I've been on
I'm finally home
I'm finally home

Left my friends and my family behind
I've crossed oceans to lay my life on the line
Faced my fears in the heart of the unknown
But I'm finally home
I'm finally home

Finally home, with my loved ones all around me
Finally home, in a place where I belong
I can finally start to build my future on this cornerstone
I'm finally home
I'm finally home

After all the battle lines that I have crossed
And all the brothers and the sisters we have lost
I'm thankful for the love that I've been shown
And I'm finally home
I'm finally home

After all the distant roads that I've been on
I'm finally home
Finally home

Some of us are fighting external battles, and some of us have war being waged inside, but aren't we all searching for home? Don't we all long for that sense of all-rightness that comes from being accepted just as we are, being loved without condition, being joined on the difficult journey, and being told it's going to work out okay?

We do. Of course we do.

This is why we do what we do.

Leave a Legacy You Love

Spend a few minutes thinking through the following themes, based on the situations and stories from chapter 11:

1. What thoughts, images, or emotions does the concept of "home" conjure in your mind?

2. Regardless of whether you ever devote yourself to anything involving homebuilding, I firmly believe that your God-given mission will somehow—in its own way—welcome people "home." Here's your chance to dream a little; what might that aspect of your calling look like for you?

12

HELP ONE

I MET MARINE Staff Sergeant Vincent "Vince" Gizzarelli in 2011, who at the time was living in Jacksonville, North Carolina, with his wife, Jamie, and their two children. Vince had been part of this country's historic first invasion of Iraq in 2003, and while he had made it home safely, he'd lost eighteen of his buddies in one fight alone. Preferring combat duty to desk duty, he redeployed just one year later, landing himself squarely in the middle of the action. He would somehow survive five separate IED explosions, awarding him the Purple Heart and a return-trip home.

Once he had recuperated, Vince drew recruiting duty, during which time his TBI revealed itself. It was to be expected; most vets who were near an IED explosion suffered some sort of traumatic brain injury, the symptoms of which can include migraines, vestibular/balance issues, anxiety, memory loss, and attention deficits. Vince was five for five on the classic symptoms and to them added the unwanted developments of a short fuse, difficulty sleeping, and near-complete loss of focus. He underwent treatment at a military hospital but ultimately was forced to retire. He returned home to the stress of raising two children, a terrible financial reality, and zero job prospects on the horizon.

And then things got *really* tough.

In the midst of their own tumultuous situation, Vince and Jamie received a phone call. It was Child Protective Services on the line, with a desperate plea for help. Jamie's cousin, a mother of three boys under the age of four, was in crisis, and CPS wanted to know if Jamie, the closest living relative, could step in. Evidently, the cousin and her live-in boyfriend had fallen into a drug addiction, spending almost 100 percent of their time high and thus neglecting the boys' care. The boys soon devolved into an existence like that of animals, grunting because they hadn't been taught words, urinating and defecating wherever they could find a spot and scavenging the filthy home day after day for any trace of food. Apart from a few cold bits of fast-food leftovers from a crunched-up bag that had been tossed into the corner, their search usually was in vain. Adding to this troubling scene was the pit bull the couple was watching for a friend, who also wandered around the house aimlessly, and who also was not being fed.

The situation that triggered CPS's involvement had occurred just days prior to their phone call to Jamie. While the cousin and her boyfriend were out of their mind on drugs and not paying attention to the boys, the malnourished dog jumped into the crib with the youngest child and proceeded to bite off the boy's toes one by one. The boy screamed and wailed until someone finally came to his aid. Moments later, all three boys were removed from the home and placed in the custody of the state.

The case worker's question for Jamie that day was a straightforward one: would she and her husband be willing to take even one of the boys in?

Living by One's Code

The three words used time and again to define a marine's code of conduct are courage, honor, and commitment, and if ever a military couple exemplified those characteristics, it was Vince and Jamie, on the day when they went from being a family of four to a family of seven. Understandably, all three of their new sons had significant physical and developmental challenges to overcome, but when there was nobody else available to help those boys, the Gizzarellis raised their hands.

While that transition was underway, Daniel was working with a radio station in North Carolina whose owners had expressed interest in helping us build a home in the area. Daniel asked if the station execs knew of a deserving family. They did.

The Gizzarellis' selflessness had already made headlines on local media, and as soon as Daniel was brought up to speed on what they'd done, he was in complete agreement that this was the family for us. The folks at the radio station wanted to garner support from their listeners to raise the funds necessary for the build, and so after a couple of conversations, a plan was hatched. The Gizzarellis would be invited to come to the studio for an on-air interview about their experience fostering the three boys, and toward the end of the interview, Daniel would pop in and deliver the news. While the surprise was being orchestrated, I was busy behind the scenes fielding calls both from a woman who owned a log-manufacturing company in the very same state as our build (go

Vince Gizzarelli, Staff Sergeant, US Marine Corps, and family

figure), and from a developer who was working on a community just miles from the Gizzarellis' rental. The first woman donated all of the logs for Vince and Jamie's custom log home, and the second donated the lot. In the end, a three-thousand-foot master-piece was produced for the deserving Gizzarelli family—on *that* lot using *those* logs—that was valued at just under $450,000. Shortly after relocating, they were awarded full custody of the three boys, counted their blessings, and began to rebuild their lives.

The Thing We Can Do

Years ago, twentieth-century anthropologist and natural science writer Loren Eiseley imaginatively (and now famously) wrote that there once was a wise man who used to go to the ocean to do his writing and made a practice of walking along the beach before his work. The story goes like this:

> One day, as he was walking along the shore, he looked down the beach and saw a human figure moving like a dancer. He smiled to himself at the thought of someone who would dance to the day, and so, he walked faster to catch up.
>
> As he got closer, he noticed that the figure was that of a young man, and that what he was doing was not dancing at all. The young man was reaching down to the shore, picking up small objects, and throwing them into the ocean.
>
> He came closer still and called out, "Good morning! May I ask what it is that you are doing?"
>
> The young man paused, looked up, and replied, "Throwing starfish into the ocean."
>
> "I must ask, then, why are you throwing starfish into the ocean?" asked the somewhat startled wise man.
>
> To this, the young man replied, "The sun is up and the tide is going out. If I don't throw them in, they'll die."
>
> Upon hearing this, the wise man commented, "But, young man, do you not realize that there are miles and miles of beach

and there are starfish all along every mile? You can't possibly make a difference!"

At this, the young man bent down, picked up yet another starfish, and threw it into the ocean. As it met the water, he said, "It made a difference for that one."

It's a well-worn tale, but its truth is as penetrating to me today as it was the first time I heard it. Listen, the world is filled to overflowing with troubles and pain, and it can feel overwhelming to know where to start, in the quest to be part of the solution instead of part of the problem. My advice, if you're ready to take whatever talents, gifts, resources, and passions you've been given and invest them in the lives of those who need them most, is this: *help one.* Today, listen for *one need* you can meet, and then meet it. Watch for *one* person you can enfold in community, and then enfold him or her. Pick up that one starfish, help it find its way home, and rest assured your efforts are not in vain.

Vince Gizzarelli can't help every kid in crisis, but he surely could help one—or in this case, three. I can't help every wounded veteran who is down on his luck, but I surely could help one named Vince Gizzarelli. My wife's patient and godly father can't rescue every wayward young man, but he surely helped me find my way, back when I was a lost, lonely teenager, desperate for a dad I could trust. Do you see the progression here? Someone invests time, energy, and encouragement in one person and that person pays it forward, investing those same things in someone else. And in the same way our home recipients' Notes of Love minister to them long after they've been covered over with plaster and paint. The seemingly incidental words of encouragement you write on another person's heart stick with them for days, months, even years to come.

If you find a harried mom behind you in line at the coffee shop, take a load off for her. Let her cut. Pay her tab. Tell her she's doing the hardest job known to humankind. Step out of your self-focus momentarily and, figuratively speaking, write a little note of love.

If you see your elderly neighbor wrestling with weeds in her back yard, offer up a cup of water and an extra pair of hands. In your service, you'll be writing another little note of love.

If you come across a man in military fatigues, stick out your right hand, offer a heartfelt smile, and say, "Thank you, sir, for your service." Ask him what his experience has been like, listen with attentive ears, encourage him with the reminder that his efforts matter, and in so doing, you'll write another note.

Day after day, seek out ways to remove an obstacle, to transfer a burden, to calm some chaos, to lighten a load, and in no time at all, you'll have built a legacy you can be proud of, a legacy you yourself love.

My favorite passage of Scripture is Matthew 22:37-39. There, we find these instructions from Jesus: "You shall love the Lord your God with all your heart, with all your soul, and with all your mind. This is the first and greatest commandment. And the second is like it: You shall love your neighbor as yourself." The injunction is simple and also wildly challenging. "You've been loved with an everlasting love," our Lord essentially says. "Now, take that love you've been given, reflect it back to me, and then direct it toward a world in need."

Indeed, when we follow those two commandments, the whole world changes, one loving act at a time. We can't do everything, but we can do this one thing. Regardless of the pain and suffering we've known in life, we can choose today to love well. We can center our lives on *loving well*.

And this much I know to be true: once we make this decision, once you and I draw a line in the sand and declare that we will let God work in and through us, equipping us to be a blessing to everyone we meet, he will delight us the rest of our days with miracles that eclipse our wildest dreams.

The Divine Adventure

I've told you what a planner I am, and yet if I were to describe the journey I've been on these past ten years, I'd have to use adjectives such as *unpredictable, adventurous, risky,* and *insane.* As a rule, serious planners like me don't like unpredictable things unless we've been alerted to their statistical probability, adventures unless we've planned them, risks unless we've measured them, and craziness of any kind. But with God as my witness, I would not trade a single step of the trip for anything in the world. In spite of the fact that God took a match to my well-thought-out strategy for this season of my life and chuckled as it went up in smoke, he has satisfied my search for significance in ways I never could have orchestrated on my own. He has taught me to trust his ways more than my own. He has shown me the depth of a father's love. He has surrounded me with heroes. And just as Carol knew he would, God has provided every last resource needed to get his divine work done.

All along the way, God has written his own Notes of Love on the walls of my heart, reminding me of his presence, his attention, his acceptance, and his care, often in totally unexpected ways. One occasion in particular comes to mind just now, involving my friend Lee Kirgan's flight from Chicago to Dallas one night. A woman plunked down in the seat beside Lee. Despite both of them being extroverts, it was nearly eleven o'clock, both were weary from the day's work, and the tendency each felt was to burrow inside a magazine or sleep. But chattiness in a personality is tough to suppress, and before the plane was airborne, the two were exchanging information about where they lived and what had brought them to Chicago that day. The conversation then moved to what they did for work, which is when Lee discovered he was sitting next to a pecan empress, the granddaughter of the man who started the largest pecan orchard in the South. Lee knew of her family's company and enjoyed hearing the back story on how it all began and how wide their reach had become.

When the natural give-and-take of a conversation opened the door for Lee to then share his line of work, he bubbled over with information on Operation FINALLY HOME—who we are, what we do, the type of people we help, and so forth. "The best part of my job," Lee said to her, "is seeing what God will do next. It has been a wild ride so far, and all indications are that we're just getting started."

Lee's seatmate asked many follow-up questions and seemed genuinely interested in all he was saying, but after half an hour or so, the conversation waned and both parties reached for laptops to get some work done. "Even though she had her computer out," Lee would tell me later, "I could see in my peripheral vision that she was writing a note of some sort." Moments later, the woman nudged Lee with her elbow, slipped him a folded-over piece of paper, and said quietly, "What do you say we build a home for a hero."

Lee unfolded the paper to find a check for $60,000. "Send me pictures when it's completed, will you?" the woman asked with a gracious smile. "And please tell the soldier who moves in that I thank God for him."

In all candor, I could keep my hands poised over this keyboard and write for hours on end of the divine interventions God has orchestrated for Operation FINALLY HOME over the years, times when we could only drop our jaws, shake our heads, and marvel at his lavish love. With each occurrence, it's as if the Holy Spirit is whispering, "Keep going, Dan. Look up, and you'll see another stranded starfish you can help."

To God Be the Glory

The rest of the story involving the Gizzarelli build is that somehow the project caught the attention of Bonnie Amos, wife of James "Jim" Amos, the commandant of the Marine Corps. While craftsmen were busily hammering away to get the home erected, Mrs. Amos reached out to me to commend Operation FINALLY

HOME on our efforts. While I was certainly surprised to hear from her, I wasn't at all surprised that she was moved by our work; the Amoses are renowned in the military community for concerning themselves with the aftercare marines receive following their service. As we concluded our phone conversation, Mrs. Amos told me of her regret over not being able to attend Vince and Gina's home dedication, explaining that she had already arranged for several Marine Corps officers from nearby Camp Lejeune to be present in her stead. I thanked her for her consideration and for their years of tireless work on behalf of our country's finest, and then we hung up.

Soon after returning home from North Carolina, Carol and I received a letter in the mail from General and Mrs. Amos, a formal invitation to join them for dinner at the famed Home of the Commandants in Washington, DC. Furthermore, a personal note informed me, I was to bring "three or four couples of my choosing" along. I stood in my kitchen slack-jawed as I read and reread the invitation. A four-star general had asked me to dinner? Whose *life* was this I was living?

Carol and I immediately got to work planning a trip to our nation's capital, and shortly thereafter, sleek black SUVs eased onto the roundabout in front of the hotel where we were staying. "Nice touch," I said with a wry grin to my wife, even as my insides were doing flip-flops.

We arrived and were greeted by sharply dressed marines, who lined the sidewalk and were standing at attention. Inside the foyer, Mrs. Amos welcomed us warmly, asked us about our travels, and invited us to join the commandant and her in the dining room. General Amos offered a touching prayer before the meal was served, a gesture that set me at ease and made me feel right at home. The meal was fantastic, as expected, and afterward, General Amos rose to offer a toast to Operation FINALLY HOME. He praised our efforts mightily and then reached for a handsome wooden box, which he set directly in front of him. He opened it to reveal a magnificent 1851 Navy Colt pistol, emblazoned with the Marine Corps logo on its grip. A gold plaque adorned the top of the box, which had been engraved with my name. "Presented to Dan Wallrath by the Commandant of the Marine Corps," it read. I had never served my country in battle, been injured by an IED, or lost a limb—who was I to receive such an honor? Still, I accepted it gratefully, on behalf of all the women and men I know firsthand who had.

My mom taught me from an early age not to ever come to someone's house for dinner empty-handed, and so after the excitement over the Colt had subsided, I reached for a box myself. Moments later, General and Mrs. Amos pulled out two pairs of Justin ostrich-skin cowboy boots, which had been embroidered with the Operation FINALLY HOME logo on the front of the uppers. It tells you all you need to know of this fine couple that they immediately stood up, slipped off their dress shoes, and tugged on their brand-new boots, which they donned for the rest of the evening.

At some point, we were led from the dining room into the parlor, where an ensemble of the United States Marine Band "The President's Own" was getting set to perform. The Marine Band was established by Congress in 1798 and as such is the oldest musical organization in the country. During their entertainment there at the Amoses' dinner, they played several songs, some patriotic in theme, all stirring to hear in person. Then, General Dempsey, who had just been appointed the Chairman of the Joint Chiefs of Staff and was also in attendance, rose to sing a song for Carol and me. "He selected 'Danny Boy,'" he said with an easy grin, referring to General Amos, and then he proceeded to do that Irish folk tune about as proud as it's ever been done. As I took in that lilting tenor voice absolutely nailing the song, I was undone by the scene at hand. My wife and I, who both were raised in the tiny town of

Galena Park, Texas, on the Houston Ship Channel, and who upon getting married were living on income of barely seven dollars an hour between the two of us, were now sitting in the presence of the second-highest-ranking military leader in the entire country. What's more, he was singing to us.

I flashed back to harrowing experiences involving my dad, who was so often drunk during my growing-up years. To feeling gutted over the death of my baby sister after the cancer had its way. To the bittersweet dissolution of my parents' marriage. To the thousands upon thousands of curious circumstances that had cropped up along the way, all those question marks when I wondered what on earth God was up to and how it could possibly yield anything good in the end. And now here I was, all these decades later, joyously married, the proud dad to two fine men, Granddaddy to four beautiful grandchildren, a grateful participant in the building of one hundred homes in thirty-one states for our nation's finest servants—a number that based on our present building pace will literally have doubled by this time next year—and one who gets to jump out of bed every morning eager to do what's on my to-do list.

On the flight home from DC, I leaned over to Carol and said, "I know God has a purpose for this whole journey," to which she smiled and said, "Oh, I've believed that since your first build. He just continues to put all these people in our path for a reason, doesn't he?"

After a few beats, I said, "I just wish I knew what was next so I'd know what to do. And so I didn't mess anything up."

Carol eyed me. "You don't really want to know. It would probably scare you to death."

I laughed and exhaled the busyness of the trip, letting my head fall against the back of my seat, and as I closed my eyes to replay the events of DC, I thought, *You're right. Some things are better left in his hands.*

Leave a Legacy You Love

Spend a few minutes thinking through the following themes, based on the situations and stories from chapter 12:

1. What thoughts or responses did the famous "starfish story" spark in your mind and heart?

2. What resources or entrustments have you been given along the way that you would love to see used to encourage or assist even one person?

3. How might your simple acts of kindness reflect the two commandments found in Matthew 22—to love God and love our neighbor?

4. What excites you about the prospect of God holding your future—one that he promises is filled not with disaster but with *hope* (see Jeremiah 29:11)—in his hands? Are you willing to trust him as it unfolds?

ACKNOWLEDGMENTS

I AM FOREVER grateful to my wife, Carol, whose support and encouragement kept me on the path God laid out for my life. God truly blessed me with this wonderful woman, whom I dearly love.

Thank you, Daniel Vargas, for showing me what true passion for our injured men and women in uniform looks like. You are a God-sent friend to me.

My continuing gratitude goes out to all the builders, builders' associations, sponsors, suppliers, manufactures, developers, and others in the building industry, who persist in giving of their time, energy, and money, even when economic reason says they should not.

To my exceptional team at Operation FINALLY HOME. What a gift you all are to me.

To Lee Kirgan, who has been as much of a mentor to me as a friend. You listen to God's direction and act on it courageously. Your faith has opened doors for us that I never thought could be opened.

To Rusty Carroll, Operation FINALLY HOME's Executive Director, who has astutely led our organization to a new level of excellence.

I want to thank my friends at the Texas Association of Builders, who saw my vision early on and believed that the men and women of our building industry could carry out this mission I had been given.

My daughter-in-law's brother Rodney Herrington helped me wordsmith my original manuscript with grammatical know-how I myself don't possess, and Ashley Wiersma crafted my story into a beautiful articulation that both tells the truth of what occurred and honors the servicemen and servicewomen at the center of all the action. Thank you to you both!

To the men and women in uniform who have sacrificed so much for our freedoms, which we enjoy each and every day.

And finally, thank you, Jesus Christ, for loving me when I felt altogether unlovable.

NOTES

Chapter 1

1. All statistics are courtesy of the US Department of Defense, http://www.mcclatchydc.com/news/nation-world/national/article24746680.html.

Chapter 4

1. At the serviceman's request, and for the purposes of protecting his identity, I have used pseudonyms both for his wife and him throughout the telling of this story.

Chapter 6

1. Brian Hiatt, "Kid Rock on Becoming a Grandfather, Buying a Plane, Why He Loves Bob Seger," *Rolling Stone*, February 17, 2016, http://www.rollingstone.com/music/features/kid-rock-on-becoming-a-grandfather-buying-a-plane-why-he-loves-bob-seger-20160217#ixzz40ZTkzISL.

Chapter 9

1. C. S. Lewis, *The Problem of Pain* (San Francisco: HarperSanFrancisco, reprint ed., 2001; first published, 1940), 91.
2. Michelle Ye Hee Lee, "The Missing Context Behind a Widely Cited Statistic That There Are 22 Veteran Suicides Per Day," *The Washington Post*, February 4, 2015, https://www.washingtonpost.com/news/fact-checker/wp/2015/02/04/the-missing-context-behind-a-widely-cited-statistic-that-there-are-22-veteran-suicides-a-day/.

Chapter 11

1. John Allen, *Home: How Habitat Made Us Human* (New York: Basic Books, 2015), from the book's introduction, location 43 of 4697, Kindle version.
2. Associated Press, "1 in 8 Returning Soldiers Suffers from PTSD," June 30, 2004, *NBCNEWS.com*, http://www.nbcnews.com/id/5334479/ns/health-mental_health/t/returning-soldiers-suffers-ptsd/#.VuIGUvkrKM8.

ABOUT THE AUTHOR

Dan Wallrath was a custom home-builder in Texas for thirty years. In that time he served on numerous boards within the building industry, including the board of directors of the National Association of Home Builders, the Texas Association of Builders, and the Greater Houston Builders Association. Dan was also president of the Bay Area Builders Association.

In 2005, he founded Operation FINALLY HOME, a non-profit organization providing custom-built mortgage-free homes to military heroes and the widows of the fallen who have sacrificed much to defend America's freedoms and way of life. Dan was named a CNN Hero in 2010 and was the guest of honor of Marine Corps Commandant General James F. Amos at the Marine Corps Sunset Parade hosted at the War Memorial in Washington, DC, in 2013. In December that same year, Dan was featured in a CNN documentary about Operation FINALLY HOME.

Dan and his wife, Carol, reside in Texas. They have two sons and four grandchildren.

About Operation FINALLY HOME

Operation FINALLY HOME was established in 2005 as a non-partisan/nonprofit 501(c)(3) organization providing custom-built mortgage-free homes to America's military heroes and the widows of the fallen, those who have worn America's uniform and sacrificed so much to defend our freedoms and values. Our troops have demonstrated courage, acted with bravery, and defended our cherished freedoms. They've given us the ability to chase our dreams, laugh with our friends, and have dinner with our families. They have given us—proud Americans—a higher quality of life.

At Operation FINALLY HOME, we believe that it's our turn to give that quality of life back to them. And that starts with a custom-built home. By removing the financial burden of a mortgage and providing accommodations tailored to a veteran's special needs, our heroes and their families can rebuild their lives with less worry. They can move around their home with ease, focus on developing a fulfilling career, and spend valuable time with their children.

Operation FINALLY HOME partners with corporate sponsors, builder associations, builders, developers, individual contributors, and volunteers to help America's military heroes and their families transition to the home front by addressing one of their most pressing needs—a home to call their own. To find out more, visit OperationFINALLYHOME.org.

Letter from Dan Wallrath, Founder/President, Operation FINALLY HOME

As I explain in *Building Hope,* Operation FINALLY HOME has already had a significant impact across the United States. While we are very proud of the work we have been able to do, we are keenly aware that there is much more to be done. With service members scattered in conflicts all around the world, the number of wounded, ill, and injured veterans in need of a home is only going to increase.

The work Operation FINALLY HOME strives to accomplish is a monumental endeavor, and we cannot do it alone. We need your help. We need builders from across the nation to help us build homes. We need developers from across the nation to donate lots or sell them to us at cost. We need building suppliers to donate materials. Most of all, we need Americans across the nation to help us spread the word. Hold events in your hometowns or volunteer for one of our events in your area. Help us raise awareness and funds to help our wounded veterans. This is a problem that can only be solved if we all work together as a nation.

OperationFINALLYHOME.org